WENDELL OXFORD

PROCESS OF REALIZATION

The Ultimate Guide to Goal Realization, Learn About
The Best Practices and Effective Strategies on How to
Realize Your Goals and Get Everything You Want

Descrierea CIP a Bibliotecii Naţionale a României
WENDELL OXFORD
    PROCESS OF REALIZATION. The Ultimate Guide to
Goal Realization, Learn About The Best Practices and Effective
Strategies on How to Realize Your Goals and Get Everything
You Want / Wendell Oxford – Bucharest: Editura My Ebook, 2020
    ISBN

WENDELL OXFORD

PROCESS OF REALIZATION

The Ultimate Guide to Goal Realization, Learn About
The Best Practices and Effective Strategies on How to
Realize Your Goals and Get Everything You Want

My Ebook Publishing House
Bucharest, 2020

Achieving Your Goals in Realization Goal Realization
Self Help Guide

At what time you honestly work to achieve your goals, there is nothing that anyone can say to you that matters. That is the exception of course, of others opinions that you count on. Some people I know have a habit of sticking their nose where it doesn't belong, and these people often make it difficult to reach your goals, especially if you allow them. That makes me angry at what time someone butts into a conversation that the person was not even a part of the conversation. There are always going to be opinions that are given to you that you really don't want to hear. However, you need to just block them out and focus on what you want to be your goals in life. In other words, you will find areas in your life where people want to voice their opinions to help you along the path of reaching your goals, and sometimes these opinions are controversial. I am going to take the time to tell you about a few goals that I have accomplished in my life so that you will be able to get a basic understanding of goals.

The first goal that I ever made was the goal to graduate. Throughout the whole time that I was in school, my mother told me that I wasn't going to graduate. The reason she said this, was that the people that I was friends with were bad associations. It mad me mad, because I worked hard to make straight A's on all my report cards and in the end it was only to hear that "I wasn't going to amount to a hill of beans." I guess she didn't believe me when I told her "my friends couldn't make me do anything that I didn't want to do." However, in the end, I did and it felt so good to prove her wrong. See all I had to do was keep my focus on my goal and I was able to achieve it with no problems. Yes, I had to struggle a little making sure not to lose focus but it was worth it all in the end. I also enrolled in the National Guard while I was in school because I wanted to be like my father and serve in the military. Those were big shoes to feel because it was in the Vietnam War but I knew that if I tried I could do anything that I put my mind too. After a year in the National Guards, the services released me on medically discharges because I had cervical cancer. However, I never lost my faith and I kept going.

That is why it is important that you keep your mind on the important things in life, everyday drama isn't worth losing grip of your goal. After I graduated high school, I wanted to go to college, but I wanted to take some time off, after all I deserved

6

it. During the time that I took off from school, I met a guy, who is now my husband and I had a baby. Since this totally changed my plans, I wasn't able to go to college like I wanted to but I was able to enroll in an online course where I could go to school from home and become a medical transcriptions and I am still working on this right now.

The point of this whole article is to let you know that no matter what comes up in your life, you can reach your goals. All you have to do is keep looking ahead and never look back, no matter what. The things that you done in the past don't matter today, they are in the past leaving them there. Dating sometimes has its own goals in mind.

Dating and Goal Realization Self Help Guide

When you enter a relationship with someone, you always have certain things that you want to achieve through this relationship; you may say that you have goals for that relationship. In order to achieve those goals you have to work along side of your boyfriend or girlfriend so that together you can achieve those goals. I have taken the time to jot down a couple of goals that you may have in a relationship, I hope that by the end of this article, you can realize the goals that you have in your relationship through goal realization.

The first goal that most couples have is to get along with each other and sometimes this can be a tough road to walk. Yet it depends of course on who you are with and what kind of person they are, thus where do they fit into your goals. Most couples fight over simple stuff like jealousy. Every couple has had a fight over one or the other scoping someone out. The truth of the matter is that every guy is going to look at other girls, likewise women are going to look at other men; it is just their natural instinct to and it is okay as long as they don't touch. It is

8

also wrong for a man to look at another woman, lusting her, yet this is one thing that every female has to learn about a guy. Although it is sometimes hard to deal with you have to learn through goal realization that in order to make this relationship work you are going to have to realize that your boyfriend or girlfriend isn't going anywhere unless you push them to do so. I recently asked a couple of my husbands guy friends "Why do you normally cheat on a girl?" and all of them said because they accuse us of cheating all the time. I just laughed because one of his friends has dated about eight girls in the last month and I know that he is truly a player, so it couldn't have been the girls fault. The point I am trying to get across is that no couple can survive if you do not trust the other person you are intimately involved with, thus a relationship without trust is useless.

Another goal that a couple may have is to get married; most coupes do this after they have been together for a long time. On the other hand, some couples do this right away. Through goal realization, you will be able to know when the time is right. You do not want to marry someone that you can't get along with or someone that you don't know that well. That is why I truly discourage marriage under a year, because I have known people that have dated for less than two months and got married and of course, it didn't work out. That is what happens when you rush into things like marriage.

Marriage takes time, and during that time, you should really get to know the person that you are planning to marry, because the person that you plan on marrying is going to be the person that you spend the rest of your life with, which means plans, has to exist.

The last goal that I would like to talk to you about that every couple has is the goal to be happy together for a long time. My mother and father have been together for twenty-seven years. I do not see how they made it that long because when I was younger they used to disagree a lot more than they got along. However, they stuck in it and they will be married twenty-seven year in June. Most people that I know get into a relationship with someone because they are lonely and don't want to spend their life by their selves.

This is okay, if you truly like the other person but if you don't, wait until you find the right one.

Well I am going to go now so that I can move ahead with my work but I hope the information that I have given you, helps you out along the way to achieving your goals.

Goal Realization Self Help Guide

Realizing your goals is an important step. If you realize your goals, you will find relief, since plans and actions will follow. Following plans and actions will comes achievement, success, and accomplishment. Realization is an understanding of your direction in life. If you understand your direction, you will comprehend what you must do to achieve. This brings you to awareness and consciousness, which is an outstanding quality bringing forth insights.

Goal realization helps a person feel fulfilled and complete.

Goals are essential. If a person does not have goals, they often feel a lack of purpose. Having purpose in life provides principals, rationale, ideas, points, reason, and the like. If you have purpose, you feel complete, since your intentions are on track. This takes you to goals since you focus on your aims or objectives in life.

Goals make a person feel as though he can accomplish, which makes the person feel motivation. The most important way to realize your goals is to setup short-term goals that work

11

toward long-term goals. For instance, my short-term goal was to finish college and my long-term goal was to buy a log cabin and live in the mountains while continuing my career as a writer. I've had major setbacks; however, I've completed many short-term goals that will eventually lead me to my long-term goal. Thus, it is important to set goals you can reach.

As you set your goals, it is important that you strive to achieve and reach the goals. Giving up will only, cause you stress, especially as you work toward your goals, it is important to ask questions as you move along. Asking questions will keep you in a reality check and help you to learn how to reach your goals.

Realization in self is the ability to recognize one's own potentials or abilities. The realization of self-alone will bring you fulfillment. At what time a person feels fulfilled him or she often moves smoother throughout their life and to the point of achieving their goals.

Goals are terminal points that lead to a race in life. Goals should be easily set and achieved, thus while setting goals you want to keep logic in mind. If you set goals out of your reach, it is likely you will never reach the end of the race. Setting goals out of your reach will also frustrate you. Thus, at what time you continue to fail you will loose self-esteem, self-control, confidence, and all mechanisms that make you a complete human being. The overall point is to set goals where you can win the race. To help you we can look at a few strategies.

Goal one: Plan to finish school

Goal 2: Plan to work to earn back money spent on education Short-term goal: plan to save to open my own business Long-term goal: Plan to open my business in five years.

While this may not be your goals, many people have made goals in their lifetime. Thus, looking at the goals consider what you think might be needed to reach the goals. The first goal is obvious, since you have to apply self to finish school. The second goal is reasonable. The third goal is good, but you will need a job that brings you in sufficient funds to open a business in the near future. Rather it depends on the type of business you are opening; however, you will need cash.

As for the long-term goal, this step will determine if you win the race. As you can see, it takes great effort to reach goals to win the race; however, it takes resources and more to make it work. Remember, goal realization is one achievement you have made in life.

Goal Realization Achieving in Life Self Help Guide

In order to achieve your goals you must possess certain qualities, I am going to tell you about a couple of the qualities in the following article.

1) You must be outgoing. You must be willing to go the extra mile so that you are able to reach your goals. Sometimes you may come upon an obstacle in your way that you may think that you can overcome but you can. No one said that it was going to be easy to achieve your goals, you are the one that set them, and you have to work to make sure that you reach them. If you are outgoing, you can do anything that you want to do in life.

2) You must be patient. You have to understand that everything isn't going to be smooth sailing and happen just when you what it too. It takes time for you to be able to achieve your goals, it will not happen over night.

3) You must be strong. You will have to take criticism well, because along your journey you are going to have to listen to what other people say and learn from it. The people that are

giving you advice are not trying to be mean; they are just trying to help you out. If no one helps you, you are going to have a harder time than most people would.

4) You must be adaptable. You are going to have to adjust to different situations and environments when you are going to college to get your degree or start your first day on your job.

5) You must look toward the sky. When I say this, I mean that you must be able to believe that anything can happen. If you put your mind to it, you can do anything that you want to. It is entirely up to you, how many goals that you set for yourself. Make sure that you don't set them so high that you can't achieve them.

Goal Realization is being aware of what your goals are and knowing what you have to do to achieve them. Only you know what you want to be and where you want to go in life. Make sure that you don't lose your way along the path, it can be very hard to stay focused on the things that matter the most. If situations arise and you don't know what to do you can ask somebody for help or you can pray about it. I truly believe that there is a God and he can help you out with stuff that you just can't seem to find the answer to, thus praying sometimes helps you to reach goals. If you pray about, he will send you the answer to your question and guide you along your way. Just remember that there is nothing too big or to small for you to accomplish. Your goals can be the most important thing in your life, they can range anywhere from having a baby to being a lawyer. You can be anything you want to be and I encourage you to do so.

Overall, goal realization is having a purpose in life. If you have a purpose, you will often achieve rather than fall on your face. We can all set goals, however if a purpose is not established, our goals are often out of reach. This is because we fall harder and stumble more along the way to achieving our goals. You need then to establish a purpose and move those obstacles out of your way. Planning is a big part of goals.

Goal Realization and Planning Self Help Guide in Goals

It is important to setup strategies for both short and long-term plans. Long- term plans are the process of producing art of invention, giving a description of what you want to do in the distant future. Plans can stretch to 10, 15, 20, or more years. At what time, you extend goals beyond your lifespan; the plans become a powerful source in which we can draw from to gain energy. For instance, we can consider those purchasing life insurance, which extends past their death. As you can see, plans and goals can stretch to death. It is important that you bear in mind; plans have no wrong or right approach.

However, if you take time from your busy schedule you can write down your short and long-term goals. This will help you stay on track.

The first step in planning is to affirm your goals in an effective manner. Your goals should include detail specifics of what you want to change now, later, in your future, and even in the environment. To start you will need to affirm your goals, starting from result to measuring. You should measure the goals to visual outcomes. You should think in detail how reaching your goals would make things different for your future. Write the outcome down. As you, write the details of your visualization down, note the changes by feeling the results, hearing the sounds, and tasting the experiences.

If your goal is to finish college in the next two years, realize that you have took the first step that gives you power by starting college and putting forth your best efforts to achieve. Now you could move into reviewing the specifics. Next, you can put the goal in psychical action. You might say aloud, "I intend to finish school in two years by applying myself completely to accomplishing my goal." If you measured your goals, it will become clear as to the efforts you will apply to achieve results.

Next, you want to keep fresh in your mind throughout the process of reaching your goals that measures differ from values. In other words, behind your goals are emotions, values, ideas, realization and so forth. For instance, if you tell you aloud that you intend to complete a course in English by the end of the semester you will need to apply purpose to value, measures, and the like. Thus, stating your purpose is idea for reaching your goals. If you have no purpose, what is the point of plans and goals? Let's consider values, ideas, measurements, purpose, and the like to determine how it fits into goal realization.

Measurements are the capacity of a goal or plan that sizes up a purpose through realization. Purpose is a reason that leads to points made in life. Purposes present ideas, rationale, principals, functioning, intention, and the usage to reach the purpose. Purpose also presents targets, aims in life, and ultimate goals. As you can see you cannot have one without the other, otherwise it will not work.

Values are principals or standards that we set to reach goals. Values back our moral, ethnicity, and ideals. If you do not have value, it will be difficult to reach your goals. Principals then are the main belief of an individual.

What do you believe that you can accomplish in life? Principal is morality and ethnics combined that help you to see through obstacles clearly. If you do not have beliefs and back those beliefs, your purpose is outweighed.

As you can see, setting goals is an accomplishment in itself. Are you ready to fight to win?

Goal Realization Fighting to Win Self Help Guide

It is so hard to keep your goals the number one priority in your life, there are so many situations that come and go that it is hard to focus at times. The difficult times are when you need to keep a stable mind and look forward to the future. Everyday is a test to see if you can actually achieve the goals that you have set for yourself. I would like to tell you how you could make your goals number one priority over anything else through goal realization.

Goal Realization is the act of knowing what you want out of life and working to achieve those goals. If you get a spare moment, sit down and write down the goals that you have set for yourself. You may notice that the list may be endless, and that is okay, because there is no end to what you can do if you put your mind to it. After you look over the list of goals that you have written down, take the time to think of what goals you have already achieved. For example, on my list there is a couple that I have already achieved. The goals that I have already met was graduating of high school, getting married, and having a baby. I have already completed three goals that I had. However, there are some other goals that I need to work toward achieving. For instance getting my degree in medical transcription and become rich. Which I know will probably never happen, but you never know what could happen during the time of your life, right? The main point that I am trying to make is that in order to achieve the goals that you have set for yourself you are going to have to work hard and you can do this through goal realization.

There is nothing to big for you to do; all you have to do is use a gift that was given to you a long time ago, the gift of knowledge. Everyone is capable of achieving their goals, but only those who have the passion will survive in this race. There are also other ways that you can achieve your goals through realization and I am going to take a minute to tell you a little about them.

Another way to realize your goals is to look into the future and image where you will be five or ten years from now. If you do not care for where you are now in your life then this will show you how much work you need to do in order to get where you want to be in life.

For instance, right now I live in a little apartment in the city limits, five years from now I want to live in the country in a nice house with plenty of yard. If I want to achieve this goal, I am going to have to save up the money and make this dream a reality. Otherwise, it will just be a place in my mind that I want to be but can't. Your dreams cannot come alive to you help them too.

Anybody that takes a deep look at their life will know that they have goals to achieve. It doesn't matter how big or small your goals may be you can still achieve them. It is just the fact that long-term goals cannot be achieved overnight. It is very important that you keep your goals number one priority over everything else. Your goals should come before anything else with the exception of your family.

I hope that you are able to realize your goals through goal realization and I which you the best of luck. Remember that sometimes the road may get hard but you can over come this. All you have to do is keep your eyes on the prize that will be there when you get to the end of the road. Goal realization can be your friend or your enemy; it is totally up to you how you choose to voice your opinion on this subject. Best wishes and have a wonderful future. I know you can do it. Goal realization swings from school to jobs in most instances, and moves ahead.

Goal Realization from Schools to Jobs Self Help Guide

The most important thing you can do in your life will be to set yourself some goals. Goals are achievements that you want to reach throughout your life. I am going to tell you a little more about some goals that you should have throughout your life. You should be able to review your goals through goal realization.

High School

The most important goal in everyone's life is to graduate. As teenagers, we think that we should have more independence and by graduating, we are able to get the freedom that we want. There is nothing like receiving a diploma.

When a teenager graduates, sometimes they may take a break from school and at other times, they will head right off to college, this leads to my next goal that everyone should share.

College

The second goal that most teenagers have is the goal to go to college and make something out of their selves. During the whole time they are in school, teenagers are worrying about making the grades to get into college, not to mention the fact that they worry about which college is going to accept them. I believe that college preparation is the hardest on teenagers, it cause them a lot of stress and concern.

Jobs

After college some teenagers go back home to mom and dad, others begin their journey through life with finding a new job. As a teenager, I love to work just so that I would have a little money to get the things that I want. Once I moved out on my own I realized that jobs aren't to buy the things you want, they are to pay bills that you will have once you are out on your own. You should always remember to find a job that you will like and enjoy. If you get a job that you don't enjoy you are going to be stressed out a lot more than what you think.

After College

Most teenagers after they go to college, get their own place, and find a new job, they normally choose to settle down and have a family. This is where all the fun begins; to some this may be the end of there teenage years for others, it is just the beginning. I personally think that settling down and getting married was one of the best things I could have done. As for my son, I love him with all my heart.

Overall

Goal realization is a process that only you can do, only you know what you expect out of life and only you know what the outcome is going to be. I hope that you have all the strength that it takes to deal with everyday life and I hope that you are able to achieve all the goals that you have set for yourself along the way. For the most, I hope that you have learned how to realize your goals through goal realization. You will find that along your journey there are going to be obstacles that may stand in the way of you reach your goals. Don't lose faith, just deal with the situation, and move on. There is no object to big to overcome, it may be tough, but you can do if you put your mind to it. If you are unable to, just think about the goals that you have set for yourself, try to write them down and think about what it is going to take to achieve them. Other ways of goal realization is to visualize what you goals are. Are you planning your life?

Goal Realization Planning your Life
Self Help Guide in Achieving and Setting Goals

What are you planning to do with your life?
Do you know where you will be in the next ten years?

If you do not know the answers to the two questions, then you need to focus on goal realization, since there are more questions to follow. The point of goal realization is to make you more aware of what you want to do in life.

Nobody knows the answer to these questions but you. There are many ways that you can realize what your goals are in life.

One way is to write your goals down. At what time, you get the time, sit down, think about the goals that you have already accomplished, and then think about the goals that you haven't accomplished yet. While you are writing your thoughts down, take the time to jot down a few ways that you can achieve those goals. By doing this you will be able to see how much work it is going to take on your part to reach your goals.

Another way that you may be able to realize your goals is to think about what you want to be in life and then work toward achievement of that goal. For instance, if you want to be a doctor, you need to go to college for a number of years. However, you may be able to settle for a profession that requires a little less time as far as education is concerned until you are able to reach your true goal. Maybe you will be able to be a registered nurse, it is just as good of a job, but it requires less education. However, the pay is less also. That is why it is important for you to plan your goals ahead of time. So that you want have to spend the rest of your life trying to accomplish something and once you do, you've done let your entire life pass you by. In other words, fit in short-term goals that work with long-term goals.

You can also talk with a guidance counselor at your local college and ask her or him for some advice on achieving your goals. The guidance counselor can help guide you in the right direction on how to accomplish those goals and how to go about doing it. He or she will be able to tell you about courses you can take and degrees that you can get. I think that talking to someone about your goals can also be of great help. Not only are you getting your own advice but also you are getting the advice of a professional so you will be able to know that, yes, your goals can be reached.

Goal Realization is very important; if you don't have any goals in life then what do, you plan on doing with your life. Goals are achievements that you want to be met on your behalf. Don't be afraid to try to conquer your goals, you can achieve anything that you put your mind too. Do not let anyone tell you different, especially someone that doesn't have any goals on there own established or completed. Because they have no more room to talk than the next person does.

Don't be the next person sitting in front of television wondering where time is going. Likewise, do not be the next person that asks five years down the road, "What happened to my life." The issues are a caustic case of problems we deal with in life everyday. Goal realization overall is the gateway to learning.

Goal Realization the Gateway to Learning

Achieving your goals is the most important thing that you can do throughout your life, which is why I am going to tell you what goal realization means to me.

(G) Getting the job done regardless of the amount of work it is going to take to achieve your goals. (Never giving up)

(O) Outgoing, you have to be outgoing in order to achieve your goals. You have to be willing to walk that extra mile if you have to.

(A) You have to have attitude, a positive attitude that is. You have to be willing to work with anyone that it takes to get the job done regardless of your own personal feelings.

(L) You have to be a learner, in order to achieve your goals you are going to have to be willing to learn new technology, technology changes more and more everyday.

(R) You have to be ready to reach those goals that you have made for yourself, if you don't work to achieve them, they will never be reached. Sometimes you have to reach to the sky and bring down the moon but you are going to have to do what it takes and you are going to have to, never lose faith.

(E) You have to be full of energy; if you are lazy then you may have a slimmer chance of actually reaching your goals.

(A) Alert; you have to be aware of the things that are going on around you. In today's world, nothing is ever the same.

(L) You have to have the advantage to move around, what I mean by this is you have to be able to move throughout different stages in order to make it to the main event.

(I) you have to remember that there is not just an "I" in team, when you are working as a team it is very important that everyone gets the proper representation for their work done.

(Z) You have to get plenty of (Z's) what I mean by this is that you have to get plenty of sleep so that you will be able to handle the stress of everyday life.

(A) You have to be able to maintain a calm nature about yourself so that you will not get angry at anyone that may be working with you to achieve your goals.

(T) Time is of the essence; try to make sure that you make all your deadlines on time.

(I) Independent, if you are one of those people that rather work alone, you may need to get a job that allows you to work on your own.

(O) Open Minded, you are going to have to be willing to accept others input regardless of you agree with it or not.

(N) Last but not least, you have to be nice, no one likes working with someone that is angry or mad all the time.

I hope that the information I have listed helps you to realize your goals. Goal Realization is never hard if you actually put forth the work to achieve those goals. I could go on and on about how important it is to achieve your goals, but I am not. Because I know that you know what it takes to achieve your goals and I know that you will be able to if you only try. Achieving your goals is only hard if you make it that way or if you rank your goals to high.

Goals are easy to achieve if you set them at a level that you know you can achieve, and once you achieve them, then you can make higher goals to reach. Goals are the steps to your future.

Goal Realization the Steps to Your Future

The steps to your future are long and narrow, and sometimes it may be hard to keep focused on your future. However, you must not give up, your future is too important to just toss, it away. The purpose of this article is to inform you, on the subject of goal realization. The purpose is to show you how much this can influence the steps you will take to your future.

Goal Realization is often hard to figure out because it actually requires you to know what you want out of life. I know this may sound a little crazy depending on what age group you fall in to, but it isn't that crazy if you actually think about it.

Most people go through life never actually thinking about their future until it is too late to; actually make something out of their selves. You do not want to be one of those people; life is too short to gamble it all away. As you go through life, think about what your values are and what that means to you. If you have goals don't be ashamed of them, work to achieve your goals so that you will be able to say "I made something out of myself, what have you done"? I know this may sound mean but really take the time to think about this…Many people out their fail to reach their goals and laugh at those that make it, simply because they forgot their purpose in life and searching for excuses to amend their lack of efforts.

There are people out there that talk junk about other people but what they don't realize is that they haven't done no more than the next person has to figure out what there goals are in life. That makes me mad, because some of us worked very hard to get where we are today and still we get no respect. In some events, we struggle harder than usual to reach goals, since many people in the world will strive to bring us down.

There are people out in the world that work six and seven days a week and are still just barely making ends meet. This doesn't mean that they are any less of a person than you or me. It just means that they may not have as much as we do, but they are still human beings just as we are struggling harder than others to reach their goals are.

I guess what I am trying to say is if you are planning for your future, don't act better than someone because you have a better job or better education than someone else does. You are just the same as the next person; rather focus on the bigger picture while applying self to reach those goals.

In order to achieve your goals you must be open minded and willing learn without ceasing. Your goals are only as far away as you want them to be. If you work hard to achieve your goals, you will be able to. If you don't work on your goals then you won't be able to achieve them. It is that simple.

There is no one out there that is going to hand you an education or a job; you have to, honestly work for it. Nothing is free anymore, in order to be someone you have to make the name for yourself.

I hope you have taken the time to think about you goals and I hope that you work hard to achieve them. Good luck to you and best wishes for the future in achieving your goals. Working backwards is idea for reaching goals.

Goal Realization - Working Backward Self Help Guide

Goals are expectations we place upon self. Behind goals are principal, value, measurement, beliefs, realization, purpose, and the like. One of the primary reasons a person fails to meet his goal is often because he fails to see his purpose. You can set goals and apply self to reach the goals, but what is the use if you do not have purpose. Likewise, you must understand how goal and planning works in order to achieve those goals. For instance, many people are aware that working backwards while achieving goals is a valuable choice. For instance, you will start by taking the outcome of your goal, keeping it in mind and work backward to achieve the mission. This is the process of working to general and back to the specifics.

This brings us to see that short-term goals are important. If you have short- term, goals that work in harmony with the long-term goals you have a pattern of realization in existence. To get started visualize self in the future, say around ten years from now. What do you see self-doing? How advanced are you to reaching your goals? What efforts have you applied to reach that goal?

To take the first step you can peer into the future to see what action is required. In other words if you plan to start up your own business in ten years what do you need to do in ten years? What is it you need to accomplish in five years? Continue working backwards and asking questions until you reach today. As you reach today, start the process of putting forth action to achieve. To help you see how this works we can setup a ten-year plan to start a business.

What type of business to you wants to startup? Is the type of business you are considering one that will work successfully in the future? For instance, if you startup a computer business what do you see for the future of that business? If you consider that nowadays people have programs, tutorials and other helpful brochures and information to help them do their own computer tech and repair work at home, you will see that the future of your business might not be to your advantage. On the other hand, if you realize e-hospitals are coming to the future and decide to start a business that works in harmony with this plan, you might find yourself prospering in the future. Still, you need to consider what you will need to achieve this goal.

In other words, if you are planning to open a business that works in harmony with e-hospital you might want to achieve degrees in this field of expertise. Once you achieve the degrees, you might work in a hospital environment for a short time to get the feel of what is involved. After you start work, you will save cash to apply to your future business. You might even seek out resources that offer grants to help you start your new business. As you can see, pulling up resources is a big part in achieving goals.

Overall, it is important that you write out your plans. If you write out your plans, you will start to realize which direction you are heading in life.

Written plans can help you to stay focused. If you preview and review your written plans often, it will help you stay on track. Written plans along with action will take you to your goals with success. Remember, you may fall back at times; however, it doesn't mean you should give up your dreams.

Now we can view graduation and see where it fits in goals.

Graduating to Goal Realization Self Help Guide

The most important step in your life will be to realize what your goals are in life. Without goals, you will not have anything to look forward to in your life. Through goal realization, you will be able to know where you plan on going in life. I have taken the time to write down some goals that you may want to accomplish during your life.

1) The main goal in everyone's life is to graduate from high school. I can remember throughout the whole time that I was in school that my parents would always say "you better graduate" and I did. That was one of my most memorable moments, the day that I walked around the track at my high school and graduated.

2) The next goal is to be accepted to the college of your dreams and head off to college. Most people go through school just waiting to see which college will offer them the best scholarships. I personally didn't go to college because I wanted to take a break from school and in the process, I became

pregnant. However, I did receive scholarships, which made me feel good and smart. Later, I ended up with multiple degrees. Thus, I continued to reach for my goals.

3) In a couple of years, you will graduate from college and move back home or out on your own. Every teenagers dream is to move out of their parent's house, whether it is because they just don't like living there or because they crave freedom. In my case, I wanted all the freedom that I could get, which is true of most teenagers.

4) Once you move out on your own, you are going to have to get a job. Whether or not it is based on your education is up to you. You may want to get a simple job for now and then go back to school and farther your education more. However, there is the chance that you would want to start working on the job that your education is based on right away.

5) After you get a stable job, you may want to settle down and start a family of your own. There is no love like the love you will share with your child. Alternatively, if you do not want children you may just want to settle down with the woman or man of your dreams.

6) Along with a family or spouse come a house and a car, along with all the other necessities that you may need. Having a child or a family is hard, there is a lot of responsibility that

comes along with it, that is why it is important to know what you are in for ahead of time.

7) Once you have completed all your goals in life, your main goal, and then are to watch, your kids grow up and achieve their goals. If you don't have kids then your goal is to grow old with your spouse. I recommend that you at least consider one child; our children are the future generation of tomorrow.

8) Then your goal is to watch your children have kids and make you a grandparent.

As you can see from the basic list of goals, many people strive for similar goals. The key is to put the goals in order so that you have a chance of winning the race without falling on your face. For instance, if I had completed college, started my career, and then work toward a family, I would have been better off. Sometimes you have to look inside to see your goals.

Inside Goal Realization Self Help Guide

We often have to look inside goals to see the realization of the goals. Goals are a part of our life that we all make at sometime or another. Some people unconsciously make goals, while others make goals with realization in mind. Still, few of the goals people set with realization in mind often fail since a purpose was never established. To help you understand realization of goals we can consider a few points that most may miss while writing plans. Some of the points we want to consider is purpose, principals, values, measures, effort, awareness, and the like.

Starting with principals, we can see that it is the first among all other aspects of goal planning to set. Principals are the most important in ranking of goal setting, since it is one of the most signified participants in the chain of changes occurring during goal progress. Principals set the boundaries, since it puts us primary in charge of reaching and achieving our goals. Still, without purpose principals are worthless to a large degree.

Measures are the distance you will set to reach your goal. Otherwise, you will measure goals by evaluating each detail of the goal. You will calculate finance, efforts, plans, and the like while appraising each detail specific of the goal. The measuring of goals keeps you in touch with the rate of progress, amount of time spent to achieve the goal, and the quantity of each step you take. You can also assess and determine while computing the overall results.

Values fit in since value places importance on your goal. It is the process of having a grip on significance while finding meaning of your goal. Profits from its own standard, yet values go this merit trait further to review consequences of effort, goals, plans and other elements results. In other words, it helps you to see consequences and learn how to find ways to make the plan better.

Awareness keeps you conscious of your goals. Awareness is an alertness that keeps you awake by responding to your plans to achieve the goals. Awareness makes you responsive to your efforts, as well as other elements that include your goal by keeping your mind open. If you are aware throughout the progress of achieving your goals and setting your goals, you will understand and grow in knowledge. You will also grasp the meaning of your plans and goals, while appreciating your every effort. Awareness also keeps you familiar with the goal and efforts you must apply to reach the goals.

Effort is ultimate, since it is an attempt to reach your goals. Effort applies exertion, struggle, power, force, and all the words you would think that would not apply. For instance, as you work to achieve your goals you will have struggles, which forces you to apply more power and force to achieve the goal. If you realize that struggles and setbacks will occur as you work toward your goals, you will setup a backup plan. Backup plans help you to see a way out at what time troubles present self. Still, efforts without purpose are a waste of time.

Purpose gives you a reason to apply effort. Purposes take you to the point of your goal, while helping you to create new ideas. Principals apply to purpose, since you cannot have one without the other, yet purpose takes the front. Purposes keep us rational, while keeping us focused on our intentions to achieve. If you have a purpose, you will stay aware to your objectives, aims, and goals. Thus, goals employ efforts, principals, measure, values, and awareness and more, however purpose is what brings your goals to realization.

Marriage Goal Realization Self Help Guide

As you walk down the altar, you may have a trillion thoughts going through your mind at that particular time. However, I think that the goals that you have for your marriage is a million miles away. That is okay for the moment but once you come back from your honeymoon, it is very important that you sit down with your spouse and determine the goals that you have as husband and wife. You should be able to do this through goal realization.

Marriage is a bond that no one can break if you have built it upon a solid foundation. Throughout the time that you are with that person before you get married, you are steady building a foundation for your marriage. Over the time you are together, you build your foundation out of trust, honesty, and love. Once you get married, you are able to build onto that foundation that you have set as a couple.

You may notice that the list of goals that you have may be endless so I am going to list a couple of goals that I think a husband and wife have together.

1) To get along with one another…

2) To be honest with one another about everything, and keep no secrets from the other person…

3) To have a steady home, so that you can raise a family.

4) To have a great paying job so that you can support one another…

5) To have children so that you will have someone to show how much you cared about one another.

6) To raise your children the best you can in a positive in environment...

7) To watch your children graduate and go through college and make a life for their selves…

8) To eventually watch your grand children grow up.

9) Finally yet importantly, you want to remain together throughout your entire life.

The goals that I have listed above may be a little different from yours, but that is okay. Every couple's goals differ from one another because no one is alike. Some couples may want to get married and others may not even consider getting married. It all depends on what goals you have in life. Since I have told you what goals I think that a couple has, let me go over a few with you so that you can get a better understanding.

Most couples have their little fights where the other one gets mad at the other and they don't talk for a while. This is very normal for a couple to do however, you may want to say what you need to say and put it behind you. Some couples continuously fuss over the same thing repeatedly and you shouldn't do that. It is not good to hold grudges against someone because you never know if you are going to get the chance to say I am sorry.

Trust is a major factor in a relationship, if you have no trust for the other person it will never last. The reason I say this is that as long as you throw something like that in someone's face the person is going to do it just so the person can say you made me do it by accusing me of it. That is the number one excuse that I hear everyday, he accused me of it so I done it or she accused me of it so I done it. This isn't the way to go, if you are, having a problem with the person you are with you should let them know so that you can resolve it or go your separate ways. I guess the question is what does it take to reach goal realization?

What it takes to achieve goal realization Self help guide

Are you planning your life?

Are you ready to take steps to your future? Do you have goals?

Do you have purpose?

Achieving goals takes effort, principals, values, awareness, standards, will, and more, but most of all achieving goals require purpose. We all have goals in life and this includes each section of our life. For instance, if we decide to date we set up goals to achieve while considering other aspects of our lives. Sometimes those goals include high expectations. Realizing your goals is an important step. If you realize your goals and have a purpose, you will move closer to achievement. Goal realization is an achievement in life all in itself. Still, it is important to set plans that work toward your goals. This is true since goal realization is a fight to win. Goal realizations often start in school, works to jobs and then moves ahead. Goal realization is also the gateway to learning, thus if you have plans, purpose and the like, you

48

have goals. Still, sometimes you have to work backwards to reach goals. Now take a moment and answer the four questions listed at the top of the page.

Are you planning your future? What are your plans? Do you have a strategy worked out to reach your goals? What are those strategies?

Are you ready to take steps to your future? Do you have fears? Do you have the ability to overcome those fears? Do you have the ability to work hard to achieve?

Do you have goals? Do you have short-term and long-term goals that work in harmony? Do you have a backup plan if you fail to achieve your goals at the time you choose?

Do you have purpose? Is your purpose obvious? If you do not have purpose, thus you might as well start asking the list of questions again.

As you can see, asking questions will promote your mind to think clearly. At what time you start setting goals for self ask questions that are relative to your intentions. Again, you need values, principals, purpose, awareness, standards, and the like to make your goals come alive. Standards are important, since it sets up the benchmark to make your way to achieving your goals. Still, purpose is the value of setting goals. Purposes give you reason to travel the roads less traveled.

As you set your goals and get your purpose in perspective, you want to start writing a business plan. Business plans will help you stay on track. Now we can ask a few other questions to help you come to goal realization.

What are your goals? Are your goals reasonable? Will you apply effort to reach the goals? What effort are you willing to put forth to make your goals come alive? Are you prepared for setbacks? Do you have plans to override the setbacks? Do you understand the consequences of your efforts, goals intentions and the like?

If you continue to ask questions, you will soon see new ideas form in your mind. The ideas may direct you on various levels, thus it is important to weigh the details and results out carefully. This will help you to write a soundproof plan to reach your goals. Realizing your goals is having an understanding of what you want from life. IT is a knowledge that leads to awareness, as you move to achieve your goal. Thus, realization is a hope. Hope in turn is expectations you place on self, therefore place your expectations at a level you can relate and work with and you will achieve your mission in life.

Realization of Goals
Self Help Guide to Achieving Goals

Goals are a part of life. In fact, a study once said that if a person does not have goals, plans, or purpose in life, thus life has no meaning. Often the people that fail to make goals, while planning to reach the goals with a purpose in place often fail to achieve. Where are the accomplishments? If a person does not accomplish anything in life, often they feel lower than others do, and their confidence is distorted. This is what brings in alcoholism, drug addictions, crimes, and the like. Still, some people wander through life with misplaced goals, plans, and purpose and may not join in such activities; still, they have no purpose in life.

What is your purpose in life? If you have not established a purpose in life, you will find it difficult to reach your goals. Purpose brings in meaning to life. Meaning is a sense of significance that places value on consequences, worth, importance and the like. Meaning gives you a general idea or an overall view of the smaller picture, which leads you to see the larger picture. Thus, what is your meaning in life? What meaning does life share with you?

Moving on, if you notice purpose and meaning bear strong importance to setting goals, yet it takes many other qualities, efforts and the like to make it happen. While you can sit and make goals all day long, you can never achieve those goals until you have meaning, purpose, principal, value, and a measuring of what you intend to accomplish.

Now ask what you want to accomplish in life. What have you accomplished already? Do your current accomplishments apply to your future accomplishments? You can also ask self are your goals reasonable.

Goals are our aim in life. Plans on the other hand, are our diagram to reach the goals. Rather plans are sketches that arrange what we tend to do, as well as preparing us to accomplish the tasks. It is wise to set up small plans and goals while incorporating them into the long-term goals. If you start small at what time you fall, it will not hurt as bad. To give you an example of short- term goals vs. long-term goals we can consider.

For instance, my short-term goal is to finish this batch of 50 articles by tomorrow night. This is a bit unreasonable, since I would have to write hours on in to complete 600 to 700 articles of 50 batches. Still, I am going to give it a whirl by applying myself without allowing room for freedom to do other tasks, or enjoy life. I can work hard tonight and tomorrow and possibly finishing by Friday afternoon, which is reasonable, thus I will make room for setbacks just to be safe. Per se, I cannot finish the batch by tomorrow.

Perhaps this will bring down my spirits because my meaning and purpose is all in vane. Not, I am still working hard to achieve my goal, regardless of any setbacks that come my way.

Now for my long-term goal I intend to write more books in the future. While right now I am working hard to build up my computer while writing articles for various businesses online, I am still working to reach my goals. Of course, I am devoting my time to service others more so than working to finish other books for publishing, but I have not lost site of the ultimate goal I have in mind.

As you can see, long-term and short-term goals should work accordingly. For instance, my short-term goals are helping me to become a better writer, make money to secure my future and are along the lines of my long-term goals. What goals are out of order we often fail in our plans.

Goal Realization Out of Order
Self Help Guide in Achieving Goals

When goal realization is out of order, we have problems. Goals have to be in order to flow smoothly. Thus, if you are planning out of order you will find it harder to reach your goals in life. One of the biggest names in the world that shows goals out of order is our justice system. IF you notice the many setbacks, failures and mistakes these people make you will see they fail to sit down and weigh out consequences, plan against plans, and the like. The government is another group of people that shows goals out of order, still the two sources struggle to make it work. Still, we can learn from the structures of law and court rules to set our own goals. How does it work?

The law works through abstract thinking to achieve concrete state of affairs. Thus, the courts join with lawyers, judges, and prosecutors to talk about case files and the direction they will go to reach a conclusion. As you can see this is a form of discussion and/or debate.

Discussing your plans and goals can help you to see areas of concern, positive direction, and the like. Therefore, you will need to practice discussion techniques to come to a goal realization. During the process of making law work the correctional department, courts, police and public work to eliminate criminal activities. As you can see, we need a structure in the plan to reach our goals that will work to eliminate problems.

As the law continues, it finds the area of origination and moves to identifying the many actors, which represent the original establishment, i.e. the courthouse. Once identifying parties are named and positioned the courts move onto follow steps of a particular structure or process they arrange. As you can see the steps can help us to write goals, i.e. we can set up originality of our goals, work to identify the goal and steps to achieve the goals, along with identifying and following the procedures to reach our course of action.

The law is structured in fragments, which could work in your interest while writing your plans. In other words if you section your plans you will find it easier to read, comprehend and follow the plans. Just like the justice system, which composes many segments, including scores of jails, prosecutors, clerks, citizens, police and the like? If you can see, the sections spread out, since all areas of the world have their own law.

To help you see how a plan is structured in fragments we can consider the law or criminal justice. The structure of the fragmented law goes as follow:

Federal where the supreme courts of a country rest > State: the appellate courts also known as the supreme courts, which are the last recourse if a problem is not solved. Federal: circuit courts where appeals reside: district court, magistrate court: State: Intermediate courts where appeals take place: Trial court is of general jurisdictions and is called circuit or superior court: Trial court of limitation in jurisdiction. The last includes a variety of sectors, such as municipal, state, and county jurisdiction, circuit, justice, common pleas, magistrate or mayor or district.

Ok, looking at the structure you can see there is order in the fragmented scene. In other words, the courts are spread out all over the world, however most times the same rules or order applies. Thus, if you work your plan with a similar structure you will start to see the realization of the plans you make. The basis of your goals is the starting point to bring the goals alive.

The Basis of Goal Realization Self Help Guide

The foundation of goals is important to understand. The foundation of goals helps us to underpin issues, set the groundwork, and establish and institution where organization takes place. The basis is the foundation in which we have a base root that poses new sources. The start of a goal is the beginning that leads to the center, which in turn leads to the heart or core of the goal.

As you set the basis of your goals, you will start to underpin the goal, which provides you strength. The strength will lead to awareness and soon you will find support for finding and writing your goals. As you start to write, the goals you will see emphasizes placed in certain areas, which will highlight the theme of your goals. Once you have the subject or topic in order you can then move on to view opinions, ideas, hypothesis, notions, arguments, and the like. If you run into disagreeing areas, you can use a linage of reasoning to decide your case.

The institution of your goals we help you to organize your plans. At this point, you can establish your foundation while associating traditions, customs, value, moral, standards, principal, purpose, and the like with your intentions. To help you see I will present you an outline of a based goal in process.

Goal:

My goal is to finish writing my book by next year on March 21, 2007:

Plan A: I will write each day for at least one hour until completion

Short-term Goal: My short-term goal is to achieve a high-level in my writing business to increase revenue:

Plan B: I will work hard each day and sacrifice things I enjoy to meet my goal.

Long-term goal: To finish the nine books in the making:

Plan: I will use plan A and Plan B to work toward my goal to write the nine books in the making. I will in the meantime work to increase my business by working hard everyday without missing the final point of my goal, which is to write the books.

As you can see plans and goals are in order, yet it needs something more to complete the written plans. In other words, I have to fit in financial obligations and earnings, as well as backup plans in the event disaster hinders me. I will also need to consider my purpose to achieve.

Purpose:

My purpose is to write a bestseller in the next few years, as well as to increase my business income to retire earlier.

Now I have meaning. My purpose sets my principals, values, and measures the distance and areas of the goals to achieve. The meaning now gives me a sense of a direction I will need to go in order to achieve my goals. The meaning thus provides me significance while placing importance on the most important issues within the goals.

Now you need to write your plans since it will reveal holes in the plans you make. Writing will also help you see gapping in logics, opposing statements, concealed assumptions, fuzzy thoughts, and the like. If you write your plan, it will show the specifics while providing you power to achieve. As you move along in the writing, begin drawing pictures of how you perceive your goal and your situation in 3, 5, or 10 years. Pictures often speak louder than words, however if you practice learning the meaning of words, the words will speak louder than pictures. If you see how this works, you are on your way to goal realization. DO you have will to act on your plans and achieve goal realization?

A Will to Act on Plans to Reach Goal Realization
Self Help Guide

If you have a will to act on plans then you have the ability to reach goal realization. Action speaks louder than words, since faith without works faith is dead. Down through the centuries we can note many characters that made a difference in our history. These people took action to achieve their goals by refusing to sit down and let someone else achieve. Action illustrates strong characteristics of a human being. At what time a person is confident people will take note and are more willing to help you reach your goals.

To help you see results of a person acting out on his intentions we can consider a few historic characters. Martin Luther King Jr. is one man that stood up for what he believed, at the same time this man stood strong, went through struggles and persecutions, yet he still acted out to achieve his goals. Martin started out in school as we all do, arriving at the University Atlanta Lab School, and moving onto Booker. Martin scored high on tests, which sent him to college at fifteen years of age.

Born in 1929, Martin graduated with a Sociology degree in hand in the year 1948. Eager to learn, Martin participating in theological seminars, at the same time furthering his education, and throughout his course of action he received president awards. This is the turning point of his thirst to achieve further. As you can see, Mr. King Jr. had a will to achieve. Martin throughout his education won several awards, and finally awarded his degree of bachelors in the Divine. Martin continued his journey in learning as he reached high to achieve his goals.

Martin Luther King Jr. overall took hold of nineteen or more degrees and was finally given the Peace Award, which no other has ever received in the history of peace struggles. This man is a fabulous example of achieving goals.

His goals were obvious. This man wanted people to recognize him as a human being, thus something that should have never been a goal in the first place. That is all men are created equal and no one has the right to judge another man for his color. Martin is outstanding in his own creation, thus making him a true definition of man.

As you can see loads of action took place in Martin Luther King Jr., life. Now ask self, are you willing to put forth this type of effort to achieve? While you may not go through the same struggles Mr. King Jr. went through, you will go through your own struggles. Thus, ask self are you ready to battle to win the race of life.

Still, you need more than action to achieve goals. For instance, a detailed and structured plan will give you power to achieve your goal and put forth the effort to achieve. While you write your goal, you can put action in its place by filling in the partial details of your plans. Thus, fill in the gaps. As you write, you should allow no room for excuses. If you make excuses, you will have many setbacks along the journey to achieving your goal, and possibly miss reaching your goal.

Still, you want to remember that the best-laid plans fail, therefore keep this in mind as you write down your goals. Leave room for a backup plan to help you recover from setbacks, emergencies and the like. Backups are endorsements that provide encouragement, help, sponsorship, support, and backing. If you have backing, you have a plan. Backup plans are essential in goal realization.

Goal Realization Backup Plans Self Help Guide

Backup plans give us an endorsement to continue our journey. Backup plans are encouragement that helps us to continue by giving support to our goals. Backup plans sponsor our actions, which backs our goals. Backup could include support or help from others, including friends, family, counselors, student resources, and the like. Backup gives us a reinforcement that helps us to stay tuned to commitment. One example of backup is seen in computer actions. A user will often backup his data to disc, tape, floppy, zip, or the like. This is to guarantee that the files will be available if something goes wrong with the computer's hard drive.

Now let's consider what we can do to backup our plans to achieve our goals. Per se, you intend to graduate from college in one year earning your degree in Social Science. Now, you've already completed one year of college to earn this degree. You realize that you must study humans in society, while deciding how individuals relate to each group of people or each person in society. What can you do to speed up the process?

First, you will need a plan. The plan should include frequenting society, talking to groups and individuals in society and taking notes while you observe. Observation through my own experiences has been the ultimate source of learning. Thus if you have observation skills you have an ability to go beyond. During your study, you will consider history, political science, economics, psychology, sociology, anthropology, and the like. You should also consider religion, since it is the ultimate source of creation to present.

As you can see studying through actions, such as observation, talking, taking notes and the like will help you pass each test you take at college. The actions will also keep you aware of your senses to achieve.

As you can see, establishing a purpose is important. Therefore, ask self why you would study such natures. What efforts should you apply? Why are you studying in the first place? Asking questions will help you see goal realization.

We can also talk to friends, family, and the like about our plans. As you talk about your plans, it will bring the realization of your intentions into view.

The key is however to hear self while talking to others. In other words, if you listen to what you are saying as well as listen to what others have to say, you are self-observing which leads to progress. If you do not have the plan in motion do not worry, since talking before the plan is in place will help you grow into the plan. Once you start talking about your desires, it will cultivate a learning or understanding of your direction. As you continue to talk, your plans will soon move to goal realization.

After you talk, realize your plans you should write them down immediately. This will keep the plan fresh in your mind. To write a plan considers:

Short-term Planner Start Date: 5/26/2006 to 5/26/2007 This is a one-year plan, which should include:

Week of Monday Tuesday /Wednesday   Thursday /Friday Saturday Sunday

5/26/2006: Talk to People Quiz   Talk to Groups   Quiz   Talk to Law

Quiz Fill in Plan

Continue to the plan up until the date you choose to finish the plan. Remember the long-term goal as you work through the short-term goal. The goal now is to finish school. Thus, you want to consider what you want to do with your learning after you graduate from school. As you noticed, the first thing is to put forth action, quiz self to prepare, put forth action again, quiz self again to prepare, and so on. The more action and quizzing you adhere to the more you will learn and later you will find each test you take to achieve your goals easier. Don't forget your backup plans. Alternatively, planning is a part of goal realization.

Planning in Goal Realization Self Help Guide

Planning is a large part in goal realization. As you plan, you should set aside time for anniversaries, birthdays, concerts, music, television, special occasions, and the like. You should also include in your plan expenses such as medical, insurance, taxes, loans, credit cards, car registrations, tags, interest, contributions, bills, and the like. This will help you measure the financial portion of your goals and plans. In other words, it can help you see how much you can invest on your goals. You also want to calculate vacations, trips, or holidays. All details revolved around your plans, therefore if you plan wisely and carefully measuring out the details you will have a better plan in motion.

Planning is preparing to achieve. Planning is setting up a plan that develops a structure while arranging to reach a goal. Plans include schedules, forecasting, arrangements, and the like. Still, planning includes more since you have to remove any obstacles in your way that hinders your goals process. For instance, procrastination is the biggest stumper that halts or diminishes goals.

Therefore, you want to consider a practice that leads you to avoid procrastination. The goal now is to prevent procrastination.

Day one of seven:

Anti-procrastination goal and plans:

Monday: I intend to find meaning of my goals so that I can stop putting off what I can do today. I realize that getting it done now is an accomplishment that moves me toward my goal, and also getting it done now takes off stress.

Day two of seven:

Tuesday: I intend to break down my goals to sections so that I will not feel stressed by taking on large tasks.

Day three of seven:

Wednesday: I intend to write a statement that illustrates my intentions and what I want to achieve from my goals.

Day four of seven:

Thursday: I intend to tell everyone I know about my goals and plans so that people will respect my time to reach my goals and assist me if necessary.

Day five of seven:

Friday: I intend to find benefits and rewards for all the efforts I put forth in achieving my goal.

Day six of seven:

Saturday: On Saturday instead of resting from my intended goal, I will put forth effort and get it done now so that I am closer to my goals. I will not procrastinate, simply because it is a weekend.

Day seven of seven:

Sunday: Today, I realize that procrastination is positive and negative, thus if I can tell me self to procrastinate, I can also tell myself not to procrastinate. I simply must learn to say no at times, since no is not a rejection in all instances, rather it is a best interest word that protects me from making mistakes.

Day one of completing my seven-day mission to avoid procrastination: Monday: Today, I will look back to see my progress. At the times I did procrastinate, I will observe the experience closely to see what results came from the inactivity. I will not judge myself; rather I will review the consequences of my inactions to see where I can progress. I will write down the facts as they present self and analyze them carefully. This will help me see clearly which direction

I need to go to achieve my goals and realize my plans.

As I move along I can see when is my best time to study, plan, and work toward achieving my goals. I will write down daily my activities, plans, etc to make room for large tasks that come along. Are you ready to plan?

We all need motivation to lead to goal realization, otherwise we fall back, and it is often difficult to get back on our feet again.

Motivation leading to Goal Realization
Self Help Guide

Motivation is inspiration to achieve. Motivation is an incentive that helps us to grow, learn, and develop without complications. It is our drive.

Motivation is impulse that backs purpose and reason. To understand how motivation develops and how it applies to goal realization we can look at steps to gain motivation.

Steps in gaining motivation:

Step One: Make a promise to self. During the process, realize your goals, work to achieve the goals and analyze self. Of course, you want to use moderation while analyzing, since you want to develop willpower, self- discipline, purpose, and motivation.

Step two: Today you will learn to recognize and take control of your discomforts. Discomforts is what holds us back many times, thus today you are going to learn to relax with your discomforts. For instance, I don't want to take this test now, gosh, I had other plans. Decide now what is important. Decide what the consequences of not facing your discomforts will bring.

Decide how not facing your discomforts will hinder your abilities to achieve your goals. Now, face you discomforts and take the test. Realize that if you put off now what you could finish, tomorrow you are one-step behind on reaching your goals.

Think of time: I don't want to sweep the floor now. I sweep the floor and find two minutes later, I am finished and the floor is clean. Think: I don't want to take the test now, this is extreme, and if you dive in without wanting/desiring to take the test, you might just fail. Again, think of purpose and importance of the test.

Discomfort is a leading setback. Rather avoidance of facing discomforts can set you back. Therefore, learn to change the mind and body to conform to your discomforts. For example, I want to take the test now so that I have room to accomplish other things I have planned after the test is completed. As you talk, sit with your back straight in the chair, or stand. This poses confidence. Now consider the aspects of taking the test. What is it that nerves you or makes you lack in motivation. If you consider the aspects, you might find areas of the test that you lack confidence, thus you can study harder to achieve confidence to master the area of concern. In other words, possibly the test has math quizzes that nerves you. Thus, study harder to learn various types of mathematical problems. Alternatively, the discomfort could be the situation in which you are resting. If you feel discomfort in your position, thus rearrange your body so that it feels comfortable.

You can also talk to self to discuss how miserable the test makes you feel. Often when you self-talk, you will find that your discomforts were a state of mind that hindered you from progressing. In other words, each time we attempt to achieve in life some force seems to hold us back. If you self-talk, you will often find there was not an issue to begin with and that you just added burden to comfort.

Step Three: Sometimes you have to turn up the volume of pressure to achieve. In other words, your test is due tomorrow, thus move the date up to next week. This will apply pressure on you to finish the test immediately.

Otherwise, you can turn down the volume of pressure and take smaller steps to complete the test.

Step Four: If you are feeling totally uncomfortable with the test and unclear as to what to do, thus you may ask for help or support. For instance, could you invite a few friends over to study and prepare for the test with you?

Sometimes we just have to write our plans one day at a time to realize our goals.

Goal Realization One-Day Plan Self Help Guide

Today you are about to work through the alphabetical daily schedule, thus putting your, to do lists in order. Some of us have difficulty planning, therefore we are going to work through goal setup one day at a time, and taking 'baby steps' along the way. Throughout the process, you should start to see how much attention or focus you place on both long and short-term goals. This is the process of goal realization.

Goal: No Clue
Time Invested Activities:

Goal: No Clue
Time Invested:
Activities:

What I learnt from reviewing my goals, time evaluation, and activities:

My findings has lead me to take action to:

To help you see how this works, I will setup my own goals, time, and activities to help you see where this is going and how it helps you to focus on the purpose.

Goal: Write two books by next year:

Purpose: To achieve completion of my books in the making: Time invested: 2-hours daily

Activities: writing until my face turns blue

Goal: Write five books in the next two years Purpose: one book is to become a bestseller Time Invested: 3-hours each day

Activities: write, rewrite, write, rewrite, review, edit, and write some more.

What I learnt from reviewing my goals, time evaluation, and activities: It takes along the lines of 10 months to one year for me to finish a novel. I have a small business in operation, in which I am working to expand. I realize that I need to find a boundary and limit in my plans. I realize this because if I do not have boundaries and limitations, I will be working to expand my business and my books will not see completion. I see that I need to assess and arrange my time so that I can work productively to continue my business, which harmonizes with my long-term goals. I see if I maneuver my timing right, I have a better chance of achieving short-term and long- term goals I have set for self.

I see my activities are in harmony with my intentions, however I see that if I write without cease I will crack up and go to a nuthouse, therefore I need to add in a little time for self and entertainment.

Now, I see beyond this, such as I have a problem with devoting my time to others rather than self. Therefore, I need boundaries; limitations and a change of mind to help me gain my goals, instead of helping others reach their goals only. I could go on with what I learnt and what I am focusing on from this test; however, the point is what do you see? Have you taking the time to take this test. If so what did you learn? Do you see how your activities fit into planning?

Now we can move ahead to A:

A: Write down on your plan what is most important for you to accomplish. B: Write down what is secondary of importance to your plans and goals.

C: Write down what is least important but still plays a part in your life. For instance, I need to purchase a new coffee machine.

As you write down the list from A to C, you will see areas of concern. For instance, it is important that I get a money order today and sent before I find my self with a delinquent bill. I also have to finish 27 articles out of a batch of 50 by tonight to meet a deadline. As you can see, I have two major concerns and two important tasks of priority to complete. What can I do?

Well, first, I have a backup plan; therefore, I can mail my money order today and finish my task by the deadline. I am willing to apply all efforts within me to achieve my one-day goal. My least plan includes having fun, yet I know this is unrealistic since it will only pose setback. Financial issues is another area we can consider, since sometimes it sets us back from achieving our goals and at the same time hinders us from seeing the realization of our goals.

Financial Issues in Goal Realization
Self Help Guide

Financial issues are a part of making or breaking goal deadlines. Managing our finances is essential in reaching goals and achieving in life. Many people go through life making excuses. In other words, I cannot achieve my goal to start college because I have no funds to pay for the schooling program.

Invalidity in this excuse is obvious, since many grants are available to all of us that wish to achieve in life. Thus, a valid statement is, I intend to find funds to help me graduate from college so that I can get a good job. Thus, we need to consider how to manage money, since money is time and time is a lead to our goals.

Beginning with financial management, we can consider a few details. Most people are pressured under financial insufficiency. In other words, they realize that they do not have the funds that they need to achieve; therefore, they spend more than they make. This is only complicating a complicated situation. Thus, I find it amazing that everyday someone tells me that a family is suffering from poverty. For instance, a family living across town from me often goes without food. This inspired me to consider a program that would help those suffering hunger. However, I stood back and listened, which I learnt that the people in question suffer because they place more emphasis on buying phone minutes than buying food. The people receive FIA or welfare checks, food stamp benefits and live in a low-income home.

Thus, the problem is they, since they are not spending their money wisely and to frost the cake, each member in the household is capable of working.

I am a single mother raising two dangerous mentally ill children. In addition, my health is dangerous since I severed causalities from incidents throughout my past, as well as survived MPD and posttraumatic stress disorder. Still, I manage to work by writing articles and running a small business. Thus I've achieved goals unconsciously, even goals I never intended to achieve.

Therefore, don't give me excuses rather start managing you money. Take the first step by stop spending money you do not have in the first place.

Step two works in sync with step one. After you learn to stop spending more than you earn, you can move onto setting up a budget. This will give you freedom of mind. For instance, if you are low-income stop spending money on cell phone minutes and get a home phone without any extras and you will save money monthly. For instance, cell-phone minutes can range from $20 and up and lasts less time than intended. Thus, a home phone without extras will only cost you around $45 monthly providing you do not make many long-distant phone calls.

Next, you can start cutting back on your bills. The previous example is a start. However, consider all your bills. What do you pay for that you do not need? As you consider all your expenses, including groceries, clothes, necessities, and the like, consider some areas where quality poses financial risks. For instance, sometimes we purchase things we need and pay for the cheaper items to save money, and it costs us more later, since we often have to replace the necessity. Thus, think before you spend.

Now set up a financial emergency plan. This will help you deal with financial difficulties. If you are in debt over your head work out arrangements to pay your bills. There is always a solution to any problem in most instances.

Now you can calculate what you intend to save for your plans to achieve your goals. If possible consider increasing your income so that you can achieve your goals on time or sooner. Writing plans to goal realization helps us to focus.

Writing Plans to Goal Realization Self Help Guide

Sometimes you have to beat the head down to get information that helps you see where you are heading in life. In other words, you have to dig deep to pry questions out of your mind; root up those answers, and the like. This often helps to develop new ideas, which puts you in the race to writing your plans.

What does it take?

It takes:

P- Preview your mind while considering your goals and plans

O – Outlines – quickly outline what you achieve from your previews Q – Questions – ask questions to resolve concerns, fuzzy areas, contradictions and the like

R – Read – read the plan

U – Underline – underline chief elements of the plan A – Answers – root for answers to questions

R – Recite – recite the plan aloud

R – Review – review the plan again R – Review – review the plan again

The start:

Step 1: Preview information before you begins reading...
Step 2: Outline what you learnt from the previews

Step 3: Ask questions to incur new ideas

During:

Read aloud

Underline important key points Seek out answers to questions

After:

Recite what you write to see if it makes sense Review what you write

Review the plans in writing again

You want to be careful with review. Although it is a good source for focus, it can hinder you from seeing also. In other words if you constantly review and change the plans with each doubt that comes in your mind, you may just beat down the originality of a working plan. Same is true with repeating. I've practiced this action to analyze the potential facts and came up conclusively with factual statements. In other words, review and repeat in moderation.

To help you see how this works we are going to preview a goal and plan in the making.

Preview: my goal is to finish 25 articles by tonight. Outline: Goal, Finish, Articles,

Questions: How much time will it take me to complete the task

Read: My goal is to finish 25 articles by tonight, which means to reach my goal I must work hard to finish the articles, and it should take me around 10 hours at most.

Underline: Goal, Finish, Articles, 10 Hours, effort

Answers: If I work hard to finish the articles and maybe hire someone to help, I can finish the task in 6 hours.

Recite: I must finish 25 articles in 6 hours instead of ten.

Review: I need to complete 25 articles as soon as possible.

Review: I will complete these articles to achieve my goal

Where am I now in the project? I am 25 articles ahead of finishing a batch of 50. I am half way to my goal, which is a big accomplishment.

Doubts: If I hire other writers to help it poses risks, in which I am responsible for, thus what can I do? Maybe I can finish the articles myself in less than 10 hours. IS it possible? Sure, it is I've done it before. What is involved? A lot of stress, tension, and brief moments of panic, thus what can I do to minimize the problems?

Review: I've completed another article already, which means I need to complete 24 articles to finish the project. How much time did it take me to write 11 articles today? It took 4 hours. How much time can I take to complete this project?

As you see if you keep reviewing, previewing, asking questions and the like you will come to conclusions throughout the process. Finally, you will see a working plan unfolding, which should boost your ambitious. Observation also leads to goal realization.

Observation Leading to Goal Realization
Self Help Guide and Test

Observe, look around you while viewing the situation. Scrutinize the situation carefully to see what you learn. Monitor your mind, words, actions and the people or objects around you. Study each detail as you move alone while examining the fine points. Survey the details, while detecting new ideas.

Observe, go into your mind, and consider what you are feeling, thinking, tasting, hearing, and so forth. Preview the information before venturing off into details. Observe closely while carefully studying your findings. Now take notes of what you have found. Write down the new ideas that came to your mind.

Observe, the information carefully to see if any ideas or memories cause you discomfort. Study those discomforts. Face them head on. Now, let your mind wander freely. Do not hold back, yet observe closely where you mind takes you. Notice your area or environment as you study your thoughts. Let go of any doubts, fears, judgments, criticism, and the like. Write down in details what you have discovered.

If you continue to observe and practice, observing you will soon reach awareness. Awareness is essential in our everyday lives. If you are not, aware you boat might arrive at the dock and you will likely be swimming at sea. In other words, your mind is chaotic at what time you are not in touch with reality. At what time the mind is in chaos, goals are harder to reach and/or decide.

As you begin, practicing observing you will soon find it easy to acknowledge, remember, and carry out your plans. Observation is the best therapeutic tactic available to us. This helps us to complete tasks, focus, and review, clarify intentions, accept, instruct, and so forth.

Intentions give us meaning, however if we are failing to observe intentions will not be clear. Thus, move your intentions to the front along with purpose and observation while writing your plans.

Moving on you can see how the human capabilities can help us to progress to a brighter future. Still, it takes you to put the human abilities in order and practice to continue using the abilities for a brighter future. If you fail to practice, you will snooze and loose all at the same time.

Other issues we could address that help us to focus and achieve our goals are principals, purpose, meaning, judging, criticism, and the like. While you might look at the list and wander what principals have to do with judging, however if you look closer you will see that it has everything to do with it.

For instance, judging is reviewing something with the critical mind. Now, you can conclude while judging, however if you overly judge you might conform to a method to achieve your goals that will not work. In other words, you have to use your feelings, senses, assessing abilities and the like to make good sound judgments. You also have to use criticism constructively; otherwise, it will hinder your ability to achieve.

Now, consider observe, purpose, meaning, criticism, judging, practice carefully to see what conclusion you draw. Consider how the mechanisms of human abilities fit in to reach your goals and bring you to goal realization.

As you consider watch, closely visualizing the qualities to see what comes from it. After you are finished, write down what you have learnt and then move toward the continuous of practicing. Now sketch your plans. Rather draw up an overall view of what you intend to accomplish. Be sure to list your short-term and long-term goals as you move along, trying to keep the goals in harmony. Goals often are, seen in record time.

In Record Time - Goal Realization Self Help Guide

Keeping records is a way to keep track of your goal intentions. Record provides us evidence and proof of our works. Records are documentations that help us to trace back to the origin of our plans. Records are also a confirmation, and a witness in itself. For instance, you could tell an officer what you saw at a crime scene, however if you deliver a report in writing it will have more concrete standings with the law. As you take notes, you want to learn to write details as they come along. It is important to keep good notes, since you want to review clear writing. The process as you begin will help you to see how valuable it is to write your plans in legibility.

Recording your plans helps you to stay tuned to sounds, data, and visual images. The qualities included in the list are what you want to develop, since it could only take you to a higher level of progress. Mind maps are also great for helping us to realize our goals. If you use illustrations to make points, it will give you a clearer view. Still, you want to use other tactics to help you develop a plan that leads to your goals.

Think:

What are you goals?

Think about what you hear, see, smell, taste, visualize, and so forth as you consider your goals. Write down what you conclude while staying alert to repetitions throughout the experience. Now you can listen. What does the introductory present? Is their a conclusion? Are there details that surround the goal? What are the words of transition saying to you? Now view your images to see what you conclude.

As you write down the information, highlight the fine points. Think of your level of interest as you write down your goals. For example:

Goal: Write a one-page essay on goal realization: Finish the essay by tomorrow:

Plan: Research, highlight importance of goal realization: write down new information and ideas.

Conclusion: Start work immediately after research and highlighting important ideas.

If you consider the strategic plan here, you will see that more is involved. In other words, you need effort, resources, and the like to complete the essay. While this is a short-term goal, it can help you to see future into your plans and goals. For instance, if you plan to write many essays on various topics you will need to learn skills.

Skill is the ability to work through tasks big or small. Skills is cleverness, thus we can see following qualities are necessary to work skills in line with goals. For instance, cleverness means you can work quickly through a task while using your intelligence to complete the tasks.

Think:

Goal: I want to become the next major scientist in 20 years

Plan: Education, effort, study, applying self, analyzing, deducing, challenge, highlight new ideas etc

Conclusion: start work immediately, check out colleges in area: highlight critical points

If you want to become a major scientist, you will need to dig in your brain to see more is needed than a basic outline of goal, plan, and conclusion.

Now on a piece of paper write down an outline of what you perceive self- doing in 5, 10, or 20 years. Take the long-term goal over the length of time that you believe you will live to see what you come up with and write it down again. Continue while observing your reactions, mistakes, ideas, questions, answers, and the like. Keep going while recording down what you come up with and then review your results. The library has many resources that can help you write goals, however your mind is also a library that can help you find answers.

The Library of Goal Realization
Self Help Guide

The library of goal realization is open to you, all you have to do is seek, and you shall find. If you have difficulty, writing your plans to reach your goals you should pull up resources that will help you to achieve. Resources are available everywhere around you and all it takes is you to put forth effort to find them. Most times people sit around complaining about the things that they have control of, which hinders them from reaching their goals. The library is one resource that should be in everyone's mind, but most people think library and scare at the thought of effort.

The library has a wealth of information, including books, periodicals, and reference guides, along with other useful items. There is no end to what you could accomplish by visiting the local library. In fact, many libraries have guides that help you to write and complete your goals. The guides often include helpful tips. The tips can lead you in the right direction. Thus, if you have excuses why you cannot find resources, you might as well hang up writing your plans and goals, since likely you are not going to reach a realization soon.

Goals are big steps we take to reach the future intentions. If you understand that goals are a big part of your life, you will see that efforts are required to reach those goals. Some people sit back, waiting for things to happen, while others take action to make things happen. Which one are you?

Let me show you examples of people that wait for things to happen and an example of those that makes things happen.

Waiting for results: A woman sits in her home often drinking coffee and puffing cigarettes. Since her lawsuit and layoff of her last job, she sits and wanders why she is still stressed from bills. Now the women received a large sum of money from the lawsuit and withered it away in a few months. She often complains about pain in her legs, which most times it is because of lack of exercise. Her house is often dirty with clothes, nick knacks and other items strewn about, however this does not concern her. She has three children she calls her own, and two of these children are still living at home although one of the children is 22 years of age.

Think for a moment and tell me what you think the long-term goal is to present. In other words, whether she likes it or not she is going to get results from her behaviors and inability to achieve.

Making it happen: This same woman has another child around 23 years of age. This young man has ventured, struggling through a chaotic lifestyle to reach his goals, i.e. to become an actor. The young man picks up a few insignificant roles in movies and decides to move to Hollywood, California. To date the boy has played in a few movies and while the roles are insignificant, he is working toward his goal and currently making his own movie. These people are my friends, and as you can see, we have goals in place for the young man, since he is working hard to accomplish while his mom sits on her behind complaining and controlling others around her.

Now sit down and think about what you see this young man is doing to achieve his goals? Ask you if you have the ability this young man have to work toward your goals. Are you ambitious? Are you willing to put forth efforts? Are you willing to locate the resources? Finally, ask if your attitude is in place.

Attitudes and Visualizations in Goal Realization
Self Help Guide in Affirmations

What is your attitude?

As you work toward setting your goals you want to affirm the goals, visualize the goals, and finally adjust your attitude to meet the goals. If you have the attitude, I will wait and it will happen then go about your business and read other articles, because this is just not for you. If you have an attitude, it will reflect on your personality and show through your behaviors. Thus, to achieve goals you have to get your attitude straight.

For instance, if you have a negative attitude while working toward your goal it will reflect on your efforts. Therefore, you want to decide what your goal is and train your attitude to work in harmony. Attitudes are how we approach people and determine the outlook of conversations, actions and the like. To help you see how attitudes are changeable we can consider affirmations.

Affirmations are statements, which describe what a person wants from life, etc. Affirmations are most influential at what time the infirm if wrote on paper in the past tense. The affirmations are also positive directed influences at what time your, affirms are positive and/or personal.

Affirmatives are awesome tools, and we see this especially at what time we think of the people that use them. For instance, actors, athletes, ballerinas, executives and many others have employed affirmatives. To employ affirmations for self you must decide on your wants. After you decide, what it is you want you can next put a description on your wants as though now you've already achieved your wants. Thus, picture you at the holding the want. Detail is important when dealing with affirmatives. Details include sense, smells, taste, names, touché, and positive attitudes.

Written affirmations should flow smoothly and share positive reflections. If you write, your affirmations down on paper, repeat the information, and practice telling you aloud what you want. To help you see where affirmations fit into changing attitudes for goal realization we can consider. First, however we must consider visualizations. What does it means to you. Visualization is the process of visualizing self in a situation. Visualizations are what can make things happen, even

98

if you are not in the moment. For instance, he visualized self-shooting tweed at golf, and later that week while playing golf, he hit tweed. In other words, visualizations are an act of empowering self, thus it is a persuasive tool to achieve.

Using attitudes, visualizations and affirmations respectively, My name is Maggie and I am a good person

Visualize: tonight I will sleep easy

Affirmative: tonight I am going to sleep without problems

As you can see this is sort of practicing to train the mind in a positive direction. Since, I have difficulties sleeping at night I am going to work with attitude, visuals, and affirmatives along with you to see what happens.

Now you should write your own affirmative to replace negative areas your attitude. Only you know now what areas to consider, thus I will show you a brief set of outlines you can employ to write your own affirmatives.

I,live healthy and work hard

I,am a fast and speedy learning

I,can do anything I want to do if I put my mind to it I,am an accomplisher

Some people may think of this as a selfish act. However, nothing is selfish about building people skills we should have had in the first place. The world tears you down, thus nothing is wrong with building self up again. Are you ready to replace your attitude?

Replacing Attitudes in Goal Realization
Self Help Guide

Replacing attitudes can help us grow into goal realization. Attitudes are personal expressions we place on self and deliver to others. Attitudes could determine what other people see in you. For instance, Charles when asked a question said, "What, do you think I am a dictionary?"

As you can see, Charles has an attitude issue, which could lead others to believe he is lazy, mean, selfish, and outlandish and the like. If you wanted to go to street responses, this person would be called all types of profane names. Yet, no one truly knows Charles and why he has an attitude. Most times when people have attitudes, it is because they are stressed, pressured, or influenced by others. Thus, the key is finding the purpose behind the attitude and working to remove the attitude to positive reflections.

Positive outlooks are optimistic thinking. At what time you are positive you are constructive and helpful to others and self. Positive thinking is also encouraging and uses affirmatives to reach goal realization. An activist can certainly convince and assure self that he has a positive future. To help you see how affirmatives or affirmations work consider.

Charles is a good man. Charles has worked hard to reach his goals and to understand his goals.

If you reverse this to, Charles is a snob. Charles will never reach his goals you are labeling a man, which is unfortunately common in today's world, labeling a man you do not even know. There is no concrete evidence in most labels people place on others in most instances.

Now what if Charles was asked a question and he said, "I am not sure. I do not really know, however let me think about it." This would apply pressure to Charles, especially in a world that expects us all to answer questions in a matter of seconds. Thus, Charles is not considering pressure, rather he is thinking, admitting, and accepting that he does not know, or is unsure.

Now say Charles is a good man and smart because he takes the time to find answers. This is part of goal realization, since if you spontaneously setup a goal you are sure to fail. Therefore, you want to ask questions and probe for the answers while writing plans to reach goals. Let's practice:

Practice:

I am a good person

I work hard to realize and achieve my goals I am optimistic

I am an activist

I am sure of my future

I am confident I will arrive at my goal at the appointed time I have set to reach my goal.

I am clear, since I have a positive attitude, clear of the path I will take in life.

The list is affirmations that lead us to positive attitudes. Still, you need visualizations; otherwise, you will not see the goals clearly. How do visuals work? Visualizations come in a few forms, including dreaming, hallucinations, apparitions, ideas, mental pictures revelations, images, and prophecy. While many people believe they have abilities to employ prophecies, no concrete facts support their claims. Therefore, we can consider ideas, dreams, mental pictures, images, revelations, and the like to understand how visualizations work to achieve goal realization and change attitudes.

Practice:

I have a great idea, which I visualized in mental pictures. Now visualize self after understanding your wants, visualizing self in the moment, thus achieving your want.

I will come up with new ideas to reach goal realization by thinking through my wants and goals. I will suggest, propose, brainstorm, plan and the like to reach a decision. Now visualize self-acting out on what you said you would do.

Sit and daydream for a moment and allow your mind to vision what you dream. Continue practicing, since practice brings you closely to goal realization by conforming, your attitude to positive outlooks and actions. You have to think positive to reach goal realization.

Thinking Positive to Reach Goal Realization
Self Help Guide to Success

Thinking positive is a goal in itself to reach goal realization. One thing I have learnt after studying human behaviors my entire life is that people expect you to have confidence, yet once you achieve the goal, some of the people will come along and try hard to tear you down. Positive thinking is a process, a goal we want to achieve in life. The achievement will help you to move along in life toward your goals without procrastinating, feeling overwhelmed, and the like. To help you see positive thinking we can breakdown what positive means to help you gain meaning.

P – Positive
O – Optimistic S – Sure
I – Insurance T – Thought I – Insure
V – Visions
E – Encouraging

Now think about each of the elements while I write a few more meanings of positive to help you grow to think positive to reach goal realization.

Constructive Helpful Affirmative Activist

Up Upbeat

Certain Clear Convinced Assured Confident Definite Conclusive

Unquestionable Decisive Dubious Confirmed Explicit Clear-cut

Opposite of positive: Negative

Uncertain Unenthusiastic Unconstructive Off-putting Pessimistic Harmful Depressing Damaging Refusal

Denial Destructive

Now we can continue but by now, you should see the point. Now if you think of optimistic you will see hope in the picture along with a bright future. On the contrary, if you see negative you will see distrust, gloomy, cynical and the like. Now think about this for a moment. Do you want to waste time thinking negative and have people judge you, considering you a depressing person? On the other hand, do you want people to see the hope you show from optimism and think, "Wow, I would like to be like him.

What does he have?

Again, think of sure. If you are sure of your goal intentions, and what you want from life, you will have the ability to persuade others with your personality, behaviors, actions, and words. On the other hand, if you think negative people will see you like so many others in life, i.e. someone in denial.

Denial is a contradicting self or agreements and is a rejection, as well as a refusal or rebuttal to achieve. If you mission is to get a better job you want to come out of denial and start thinking positive. Let me demonstrate the results of a pessimistic personality to help you see that the definitions share concrete facts.

A young boy ongoing thinks pessimistic. Throughout his life, he is unable to set goals, make plans to reach the goals and achieve in any area in life. His pessimistic attitude reflects on his own mother as well as others, thus mom in time decides let him live and learn. The child is booted from school, and walks the streets day and night with his friends. He has a criminal history, and the friend he hangs with is causing the police to observe his every move. Instead of seeing why the police are watching his friends and self, he continues to make excuses, blame, and accuse. Thus, this person is filled with guilt, doubt, selfish inclinations, hate, fear, criticism, judgment, and the like. He is weighed down.

Now think of pessimistic people you know. How do these people affect you? What are these people doing with their lives? What does their history tell you?

Now move ahead and reread the definitions of positive thinking and consider self. Are you positive? Do you always have troubles in your life? Do you see results of your actions to achieve? Do you have accomplishments to show for your efforts? Continue thinking until you develop a positive mind to achieve and reach goal realization. Stress conceals goal realization.

Stress Concealing Goal Realization
Self Help Guide to Achieve

Stress is a large problem in society, since overwhelming stress will cause a person to miss seeing his visions or goals. Stress is a fact we all must face at one time or another. In fact, stressors target each one of us everyday. Yet, our ability to deal with stress determines our success. Stress is nothing more than changes. If you cannot accept change then you will be loaded down with stress, which conceals your goal realization.

Most people believe that stress is negative energy that destroys the human mind. However, stress can send positive results, including negative stressors, such as death, financial burdens, illnesses, injuries and the like. For instance, if a loved one dies of cancer it should promote the survivors to work harder to avoid cancerous elements. Financial burdens should promote you to take action to eliminate debt. Illnesses should move you to work toward health and helping others to avoid the same illnesses. Injuries should move you to try harder. It depends on the injury, but any injury shares possibility of recovery. For instance, I was informed I had six months to live from internal injuries.

Instead of sitting down and waiting to die, I told the doctors and showed them better that it is possible to survive internal injuries. I went to the gym worked out, and pampered self often afterward. It was not long I was feeling healthy again and the muscles that sagged from the injuries firm and tone.

Nine and one half years later, I am sitting on my bed, watching television and writing goal realization to you. Do you see where positive could take you? I discovered that many people that have internal injuries could live if they only think positive and put forth effort to live.

Now that we considered negative incidents leading to positive thinking, we can move to consider positive actions leading to negative results. For instance, if you purchase a new home, which could be an area of your goal, you have achieved. However, along with the new home come financial obligations, other responsibility, and the like. You are on a venture so to speak, since now you have to worry for the next 10, 15, 20 or 30 years if you can repay your debt. As you can see stress is in the scene, yet it is how you deal with the stress that determines you faith. If you were smart, you would have written a plan to achieve goals, and in that plan would include backup strategies in the event you should fail after reaching your goal, or while working to achieve your goals.

To help you see how positive thinking works along with dealing with stress by relating to the stressors that come your way. My son was recently, diagnosed with diabetes. I survived a mother that died of this disease, thus this could have torn my heart into and shattered my future. Instead of thinking of what the disease could do, I accepted the diagnosis. There is nothing I can really do, only hope that he follows the doctor's instructions to maintain health. Now think for a moment of a similar or different stressful event in your life. What did you do? How did you work through the situation? What were the results?

Thus, stress is a concealing of goal realization. Therefore, you have to work hard to deal with stress, since it is a part of our lives. Thinking can also create stress, therefore consider how you perceive, interpret, and label each time you think. You need to setup a goal orientation to reach goal realization.

Realization and Goal Orientation
Self Help Guide in Achieving Goals

Goal orientation is our direction in life. Orientation takes place to help us see the course we will take to reach our goals. Orientation also provides us point of references to consider while writing plans to achieve goals. Thus, exploiting your compass reading to write goals can help you move along smoothly.

Goal realization helps us to see our next move or steps to take to achieve the goals. If you realize your goals, you will find it easy to achieve. Realize however takes skills, abilities and qualities. If you realize your goals then you will understand details and what efforts are required to reach the goals. Thus, you will comprehend each effort, detail, and reality of achieving the goal.

As you understand your goals, you will also become conscious of the goals and appreciate your efforts in achieving the goals. Setting up orientation is the start of grasping the meaning of your purpose, intentions, and goals.

Apprehending your goal will keep realization recognition in order while you take in each detail specific of the target. Orientation is the process of making your goals real, while fulfilling a need within you. Once you realize your goals, you can move forward to accomplish the goals.

As you move along to accomplish your goals, you will carry out many actions. As you start putting forth efforts, you will look back and notice your fruitions.

We all need to fill a sense of completeness. Completeness comes from effort. To achieve completeness you must work hard, work in depth and breadth to make it happen. Once you start to fulfill you pure needs you will feel richness. Yet, you need an open mind to accomplish this goal.

Open mind means you are willing to listen although it may not be what you want to hear. If you have, an open mind you can find meaning in nearly any subject imaginable even though it does not make sense now. Thus, this brings us to developing our perceptions, judgment, and interpretations.

Perceptions alone give you insight, awareness, and help you to view opinions and the like carefully. Interpretations bring in an understanding of our purpose and intentions. Interpretations help us to explain thoughts, actions, and words, as well as conversations. The ability to interpret helps us to analyze our situations carefully while construal the details.

As you start goal orientation, you will find the following steps easy. Goal orientation is setting up a meeting with self. Once the meeting starts, you begin asking questions and seeking answers while learning new ideas. As you can see, resources are necessary, since a single person does not always have answers. Therefore, what are your resources? Do you have support? Do you have the ability to pull up resources to help you find answers?

To help you think of resources we can consider libraries, Internet, friends, family, peers, counselors, and the like. Is it possible you can use any of these resources to help you develop new ideas? Are you willing to put forth the efforts to use the resources and consider what you learn?

Once starting goal orientation, you can take notes. This will help you to recall details of the goal. This brings us to see we need to learn strategies in taking notes to help you get the most out of what you write. Once you sit down and meet with self, make sure to visualize, affirm your intentions, and work toward a positive attitude. Each step you take to better self will only lead to goal realization and purpose of the goals. Finally, writing statements can help you reach goal realization.

Writing Statements to Goal Realization
Self Help Guide

Writing statements could not only help goal realization to come to the front, it can also help you build qualities that are necessary to reach goals. To help you develop qualities while working toward goal realization we can consider a test.

Try not to panic, since this test is simple. The test will compose of "I will" and will score according to your answer.

Test Score:

1 Point per statement: No, I never do this, or rarely is this true of me 2 Points per statement: rarely is this true

3   Points per Statement: the statement is true sometimes or at most half of the time

4   Points per statement: this is true most times

5   Points per Statement: this is true most all times, or at least the majority of time

Put a 1 to 5 in the box to the left, thus the first series of test is for motivation. The second is time, and memory.

Motivation Test:

I review my goals daily and feel motivated as I consider the details.

I know what I want from life and my goals

I take pleasure in learning new ideas and seeing how they apply to my goals

I take great interest in tasking high-priority efforts to achieve my goal

I put the low priorities to the back and work on the most important issues first

I am happy of my efforts already completed to achieve my goals

I am happy with my progression to move ahead

I am in control of my life and thinking

I control my financial situations and have a budget setup to reach my goals

I am excited at the goals I set for self and assure that I can reach the goals

I am clear of the path leading to my goal

Total Score Points for Motivation.

Time Test:

On occasions I improve my goals, both long and short-term goals

I use resources often to achieve my goals

I have a support team to help me reach my goals

Each day I plan to reach my goals

I have a work schedule, which includes activities, vacations, family time, and the like

Each day I place priorities at the top of my schedule to complete first

Often I review my plans to look for potholes

I plan my activities, entertainment and recreation time around my goal plans

I adjust my timing often to make room for my plans and goals

I work a daily plan to make time for all demands in my life without interfering with my goals

Total Time Scoring

Memory Test:

I have the ability to relate with new ideas from my experience, learning, etc.

I am self-assured and confident that I can recall or remember details of my goals each day

I have ability to ponder or brainstorm when I cannot recall details

I can remember names

Important information is easy and clear for me to remember

After reading, listening, hearing I can recall and remember details and can summarize the details

Under stress I can remember what to do

I employ tactics that help me each day to remember

Memory Test Scoring:

Now add up your total scores and review the information. As you review the information, consider areas you can improve. Once you review, analyze areas that you will need resources to improve your scores. Each week take the test again to see how much improvement you have achieved.

Acknowledge the information to see how building abilities, skills, and qualities can help you reach goal realization. In conclusion, knowing self is a start to goal realization.

Knowing Self to Reach Goal Realization
Self Help Guide

When you know self, you have an advantage over millions in the world, since you will have an understanding of goal realization. To begin the process of knowing self will take you to realization of what you want from life. Thus, a basis needs establishing to start the process of knowing self.

Once you set the foundation, you will soon react to responses.

Still, you need to write down the basis of your wants. For instance, I want a degree in biology. To get the degree I need an understanding of environmental sciences, ecology, and natural sciences. Ecology takes me to learning ecosystems, natural balance, conservationism, green politics, and environmentalism. Now think is biology degree what you truly want to accomplish.

Sometimes we plan to do some things in life that later we find we did not want to do in the first place. This is lack of knowing self and lack of awareness of our intentions and purpose in life. Now sit and think of your purpose? What is the reason I want the degree in biology? Do I have skills, abilities, talents, personality traits and the like that conform to biological works? If not can, I develop these qualities. Once you finish you might find that a biology degree is not truly in your nature. Do not worry, since this happens often. However, you have a head up on your next decision. As you analyzed to see if you had qualities, a true desire, and the like, you should take notes, which will point you in a right direction.

To help you see how this works I will write potential goals, analyze the goals and go in a bit of depth to see if the goal is truly meaningful to me.

I want to become a psychoanalyst. What does it take? What is a psychoanalyst and what does he do? Do I have those skills, abilities, talents, etc to perform sufficient job while analyzing?

Evaluating the goal and self:

Hum, a psychoanalyst is overall a therapist or analyst. What does psychoanalyst do? Ok, a counselor differs from a psychoanalyst to a large degree. A psychoanalyst analyzes by using methods to discover telepathic phenomena. After discovering his findings, he then treats patients with emotional disorders by involving management sessions by allowing the patient to talk freely about his or her individual experiences. The topics often focus on dreams or early childhood memories. Interesting, but what else do these people do? Most
120

psychoanalyst study more than treat patients and will often induce theories, logics, actions, disorders, mental illnesses and the like into self to analyze more thoroughly.

Well, I have a basic summary of a psychoanalyst and what it takes to be a licensed analyst, as well as what these people do. Now, I need to consider if I have the skills, abilities and the like to achieve this goal and adhere to the strategies employed to treat patients.

Hum, I do have these abilities. I have exclusive and concrete facts along with examples that show clearly my skills, abilities and the like. I am analytic, self-inducing, and have the ability to see what many others cannot see as a possibility. Yes, I do have what it takes to become a psychoanalyst.

Yet, what is my purpose? Hum, I enjoy helping others. I am considerate, strive for facts, hunger to heal, and love human beings as a whole. Is this a purpose? No, it is an indication that I can achieve by receiving this degree, but by no means is it a purpose. I have to have a purpose after discovering self before this can work. What is my purpose?

Now write down what you think you would like to do. Go further than the example by exploring your purpose and finding meaning in what you want. Asking for help can help you establish an identity, plan and reach goal realization.

Asking for Help to Reach Goal Realization
Self Help Guide

Sometimes we simply have to ask for, help to reach goal realization. Asking for help is not bad; rather it is a commendable quality. Friends, family, peers, school counselors, and the like could give you valuable advice on setting goals and realizing what you want from life.

NOTE: Do not be misled: Some people take longer than others to establish their goals in life. Since learning self is the first part of achievement before establishing goals, we can see it takes a length of time to learn self. While people can give good advice, some can cause you to jump track, especially if you do not have the ability to weigh through the advice. I have seen people take what others tell them, do it, and later find themselves unfulfilled. Therefore, take the advice and use it if it works toward your goal, and leave the rest alone. This brings us to see that avoidance of criticism and making your own choices is required while asking for help.

You can also use resources to find help in setting your goals and learning self. Resources include libraries, Internet, bulletin boards, newspapers, periodicals, magazines, books, and the like. Possibly, you could take out a book from the library that helps you to develop qualities to conform to your plans in life. Perhaps you could read books that help you learn how to write plans. The library and Internet has many helpful guides, tutorials, tips, and hints that could help you develop your plans.

Asking for help includes digging up resources. To help you see how resources could benefit you we can consider the start of a plan. To start a plan you will need the ability to draw diagrams, maps, tables, charts, sketches, graphics, and the like while arranging the details in order and working to prepare a soundproof plan. As you work through the process, you will soon discover purposes, which are important to achieve goals. You will also learn to prepare and find your intentions through your designs. The illustrations, figures, and drawings you create will soon develop structure while showing detail specifics.

What details mean to plans? Details are features that present aspects, points, elements, facts, factors, and facets. Details provide specifics, particularize, lists, and itemize the plans. If you learn to specify you can soon learn to identify with your plans. Since specifics gives us itemized points that soon spell out what we want, it can help us to see what qualities we need to develop to reach the goals. While you may find solid evidence that leads you to believe you've discovered what you want, do not be surprised if later you find there is more needed. Thus, after the plans are written start working toward the goals, however review your plans often to see if your wants are listed accordingly.

Do not feel upset if you alter or change, or refine goals. Sometimes we do this with long-term and short-term goals. Refinements are not a problem. Rather, refinements are modifications where minor changes occur. The process is only enhancing your goals, by fine-tuning the details.

You want to consider your goals daily. Thus, if you have to refine then it is ok. Some people after discovering self and goal realization feel threatened when they unearth problems in the plans. No problem, refine, and you are fine.

NOTE: Asking for help is the process of letting others know you are considering plans that work toward goals. Do not feel ashamed to ask others to assist or aid you in the plans. Noting is wrong with lending a hand, since it provides relief. Planning life is the start of goal realization.

Planning Life to Goal Realization
Self Help Guide

Planning life is a start in reaching goal realization. You must clarify the direction of life in which you want to go in an overall fashion before realizing your goals.

Once your direction is clear you will find it easy to set goals. The best way to deal with learning your direction in life is studying self inwardly and working out. First start with values, what are your values, and what does these values mean to you. As you consider values, you will also see principals, standards, morals, ethnics, and ideals come into focus. As you begin to see the qualities you will soon discover meaning, worth, importance, and learn how to asses each quality. Now ask which qualities are most important to you.

Moving along you will see new ideas come to focus. Now, sit down and relax while visualizing self in the next ten years. What do you see self- doing? Visualize self in the next twenty years, and again note what you see self-doing. Moving along, visualize self in the next fifty years and once more consider observing what you are doing.

Now ask questions. Do you see meaning of what you visualize? Do you see a purpose in the visualizations? Do you see consequences? Look at an example of a bad plan with me for a moment to see if you can see value, standards, principals, consequences, and the like.

Plan: I visualize self-robbing the liquor store on the corner to earn money to survive.

This sounds like a ludicrous plan, in which it truly is, however realize that people actually make these types of plans and carry out their thoughts.

While analyzing the plan you can see that plans, values, principals, ethnics, standards, and the like are distorted. If you see through the plan, you will notice that the consequences are fines, court fees, prison, and victim compensation. Where does this take the person once he is out of jail and/or prison? His future holds a label, judgment, and inability to trust. In other words, people are not going to trust this person although he did his time. The future is bleak.

How could this situation turn positive? Well, once he does his time and pays for his crime he could learn from his lesson, setup-working plans that make his future better regardless of how people view him. It happens all the time.

The point is planning a life is essential and to plan the life you must look at all details of the plan, including consequences both long and short-term.

Now we can visualize another plan with less drama to see what it shares with our person.

Plan: I visualize self in the future helping abused children heal and find relief.

The standards, values, principals and the like are charitable and unselfish qualities, thus it presents a good working plan. The consequences could lead to frustrations, sadness, depression, and the like, especially at what time you connect with children who have been robbed of their childhood and traumatized. Still, the positive is you can work with these traits and make the children's lives better by donating time, money, and the like to help aid in recovery and find protection. The overall consequences are rewarding and fulfilling.

Now you sit down, write a few plans, and discover the details while analyzing your findings. Take notes on what you learn and connect the dots to see if you can find you to achieve goal realization. Continue by writing ten plans to start and work through each plan until finally you discover your best qualities. Now, consider what benefits you could gain by exploring the qualities further and using them. Career planning is a big step in goal realization.

Career Planning in Goal Realization
Self Help Guide

Resources, such as materials in writing can help you decide which career you want to consider for your plans. To help you decide on your career we can consider a few types of careers and what they could offer you.

Careers: Wildlife Fisheries Dance

Airway Science Urban Affairs

Water Utility Operation Third World Studies Psychoanalyst

Building Construction Technology Liberal Studies

Fitness and Health Nursing

Doctor Lawyer Judge

Law Enforcement Sculpture Paralegal Studies

Retail Management Substance Abuse Counsel Transportation Technology Medical Record Service Music Therapy

Dietetics Botany

Classical Languages

Stopping here, we can see the majority of the list could bring forth grand rewards for our future. However, we have to look at the involvement of the careers to see if we want to commit this type of time.

Wildlife Fisheries: overall Wildlife Fishery experts study and practice management, ecology and conservational biology to learn more about the animals and help protect the creations: The purpose of each study varies, however ecology is the process of studying natural sciences, ecosystems, green politics, conservationism, environmentalism, and so forth while seeking a natural balance.

The career shows great rewards, yet we must consider what our purpose is before deciding if the job is right for you. To help you along you might want to read and study more into detail on each career to learn what the experts pay take is, what is completely involved and more. Thus, the point is, studying careers could help you decide which direction you want to take in life.

As you can see through each career, you could learn loads of information that helps you to advice. For instance, if you choose to study paralegals you could land self in a lawyer's position in the near future. Of course, cops according to them take home around $25,000 each year, while higher law enforcements take home more pay. The point is if you enjoy helping people and not concerned about money, thus you could take on this position and find rewards. However, remember the consequences before deciding what is right for you.

Music therapy sounds nice, since it involves healing. This career however takes a strong belief, since if you do not believe in something it likely will fail you. The most times it fails are because a person does not try hard enough to discover the facts. Music after careful study, I have found does heal the soul to a large degree. If you become music therapist there is no stopping at this point, since you could move into any mental healing environments later.

While we can see a list of careers and a bit of details can lead us in the right direction to deciding a career, more is involved.

Career decisions involvement:

Do I want to further my education after receiving my degree? What resources can I draw on to help me decide my path?

Will researching each career help me to gain insight and find my purpose? Could I choose a minor of complimentary of my major study? In other words, could I take classes unrelated to my current major to help me gain insight of my purpose?

Would inventing a major help me to visualize my future? If I choose from instinct would I feel regret later?

Do I have the right to change my mind?

Question number one is on you. Personally, I am a person that could stay in school for the course of my life. Therefore, teaching might be in my best interest; however, I have no purpose to go in that career. Still, it poses good advances if I choose to do so. Now, I want you to sit down and relax while searching your mind to find answers to each question. Analyze, preview, review, and take notes and the like as you move along. Changing habits can also help you to grow.

Changing Habits to Reach Goal Realization
Self Help Guide

Sometimes we have to change our habits to reach goals or to realize what our goals are in life. Habits are often created, i.e. habits are customs, routines, practices, traditions, conventions, and patterns. Habits are also tendencies, preferences, inclinations, likes, leanings, and fondness.

Habits are addicting, problematic and lead to dependency. Thus, changing habits can sometimes work in your favor. To help you learn your habits, let's sit down, relax, and do a checklist.

My habits:

Smoke Drink Isolate Workaholic

Loyal to Breakfast Pull hair

Sometimes jump to react

While this is my set of habits, we can see that several of the habits are harmful and could stop me from reaching my goals. Still, I have achieved many goals and have achieved goals I did not intend to achieve; I still have other goals to achieve. How can my habits hinder me? As you can see drinking is not bad, but I went to drinking obsessively it could hinder my progress. Therefore, I want to monitor my actions and habits to make sure I do not exceed my limits. Of course, I do not drink everyday, but if I was to stress out it could lead to a day of drunk. To avoid that again I need to monitor my moods, habits, and feelings before drinking.

Sometimes I isolate self, which is not all bad. People can hinder us from reaching our goals still we need moderation. Thus, I plan days and visit friends, go canoeing and the like so I do not feel a threat of my habit.

Smoking is my worst habit, since smoking can affect my health; therefore, I need to work toward stopping the habit. I can do this by practicing new habits that are healthy.

Workaholic poses no threat to me, since I am working hard to reach my goals and have boundaries that I adhere to. Sometimes I jump to react which is a habit I want to work on since it could cause problems.

As you can see, analyzing and evaluating your habits can help you come to realization. Still, one you note the habit it takes working to eliminate, minimize, or else enhance the habit to work in your favor. For instance, my new habits are to eat a hot breakfast each morning. This is a good habit since it promotes health. Not anything that promotes health is a bad habit. Therefore, I can enhance this habit to work on my diet, which could help me loose ten pounds in the next month.

To help you get started and after you write down your habits start telling the truth. If you stumble upon a habit you were unaware of, instead of feeling shocked, accept the habit. If the habit is bad, you want to be honest with self. After you pass honesty, learn to commit self to innovative behaviors. If you practice a new healthy habit, promise you that you will use the habit for here to the course of your life.

Next, move to affirm your new behaviors and intentions. You can do this by visualizing self-acting out on your behavior. Notice the consequences as you see through the changes. If you fear, changes start small and work up to the big changes. This will help you set a pattern, which you can relate.

Next, ask for support or feedback to help you understand the changes. Get help to aid you in seeing the realization of your habits. The last step in learning, developing new habits and the like is to practice each day your new habit and avoid reproaching self. This will help you grow to goal realization. Get your ideas in motion.

Ideas Leading to Goal Realization
Self Help Guide

Ideas are dreams or thoughts that help us to see beyond the here and now. Ideas provide us images that lead to new ideas. As you learn ideas, you will develop opinions, judgments, beliefs, feelings, views, and the like. This will help you to develop healthy qualities that will lead you to success.

To help you understand each quality you will acquire and help you see how it can bring you a step closer to goal realization we can consider feelings first.

Feelings are emotions. Rather feelings stem from the emotions and often include sentiments, moods, and reactions. Now, if you have positive feelings you will react appropriately to your situations. Feelings also are sensations, which help us to use senses to make decisions. Sometimes feelings are sensitive, which is ok. However some people numb their senses conforming to society rules, standards etc, thus the feelings do not share root meaning.

Feelings are sometimes opinions, or point of views. Feelings leave impressions while we express our beliefs through these emotions. Feelings are also consideration that shows affection, concern, regard, love, sympathy, and the like. When feelings work in our favor in an extreme action, thus it could show through your behaviors by expressing suspicion, hunches, intuitions, ideas, and gut reactions.

The clue is visible between the fine lines. If you learn to develop healthy emotions and feelings and use your inborn senses rationally, you will develop working people skills that are required to reach most goals.

Judgments can work in our favor or against us just as emotions can. Judgments are rulings, decisions, findings, verdicts, sentence, conclusions, and results. Judgments are also opinions, views, and feelings, considered opinions, way of thinking, reason, beliefs, assessments, and the like. We can use judgments to discriminate others and/or self, which are unhealthy and will only blind our minds to seeing our goals. We can also use our judgments by adhering to common sense, wisdom, or intelligence. Sometimes we even call for shrewdness while judging self and others, therefore learn to put your judgments in place to avoid problems.

Opinions are something you want to consider closely. Too many people today and in our history give opinions that do not present facts. Thus, if you give opinions you want to develop your beliefs by showing facts. This is an example of judgment. If you offer opinions or set goals based on opinions that have no concrete evidence to support facts, you are illustrating negative judgment. Thus, state the facts. Opinions also help us to see outlooks of situations, plans and the like. Accordingly, you want to watch closely while giving opinions.

Beliefs are stronger than opinions, since many beliefs share faith, convictions, principal, and ideas. Beliefs also share confidence, trust, certainty, credence, and so forth. To help you determine or weigh out opinions you can consider what you believe and trust.

For instance if you spot an opinion and/or someone gives their opinion you should watch for disbelief, doubts, suspicions, mistrust, misgivings, and trust. You should listen to your suspicions, doubts, disbeliefs, and the like and while skeptical, you should work to find facts that support the opinions. This will help you develop healthy qualities, which will lead to goal realization.

As you, notice-developing qualities that work toward a positive direction are the steps in reaching goal realization. If you fail to develop your qualities, it will only hinder you in life. Still, it is important to write down your new findings and practice each day to put on that new personality. A winning personality can't loose, since they often find goal realization. Exploring is part of finding goal realization.

Exploring to Find Goal Realization
Self Help Guide to Success

Exploring self is a surefire way in finding your goals. Exploring self however extends to exploring new ideas, old ideas, and opinions from self and others to find realization. To help you see how exploring works we can consider an opinion. The philosophers, theorists, opinionated people in the world often believe we evolved and that we are half animals. This is a bona fide lie, yet they will claim they have evidence to support their claims. All the while as they make their claims new information comes available that points to creation. What do you believe? What if it were true that we evolved and are half-animal? DO you have facts to prove your claims? IS there evidence that supports you logic?

As you can see, you have to dig in the brain to come up with conclusions, as well as check references and resources to find facts. This helps you open the mind and promote awareness that leads to goal realization.

Still, if you find answers it does not mean it is true; therefore, sometimes you have to keep digging to find new ideas. Now to discover your learning patterns you have to discover your purpose of learning. You also have to unearth meaning and discover how it applies to your life. Furthermore, you have to experiment while learning to find meaning, purpose, and relation. Once you understand learning, you will move to using what you learn to apply to your goals. As you can see this fits in well with exploring, since you cannot have one without the other. This brings us to critical thinking, which is a part of exploring self, goals, and the like. To help you see how you form critical thinking tools that are in the mind already we can adhere to a practice.

Understand ideas are mechanisms or tools that help us to discover. Moving along I want you to describe an area of your life when you had a problem. The problem could be adjusting to a new relationship, getting over a lost relationship, battling school tests, and so forth. You can also explore smaller problems if you like. I will work with you, show you one of my problems, and show you what I concluded. As you move along look at the changes and how they affected you. Consider the consequences and new ideas that came from the situation.

Practice:

Problem: My child refuses to listen to me and hangs with the wrong crowd, smoking, possibly taking drugs, and drinking.

Ideas: My son is seventeen and was taught better, thus his influences are a part of the problem. I have tried my best, thus it is time to let him live and learn.

Solution: I will let him live, learn, and at the same time enforce the rules while seeking out other solutions.

Consequences: I may have to deal with my son going to jail and dealing with court costs while people may look down on me.

Solution: I don't care what others think of me because most people in my neighborhood know I've done my best. As for jail, maybe it will lead him to his senses. Court fines are optional, since he is seventeen and now considered an adult.

Ideas: I will continue my life and stop worrying about what I cannot change and do something about what I can change.

While there is no conclusion here, I see that areas of my child raising, presents issues. While I've done my best somewhere along the line I made mistakes. I need to consider **Exercising to Explore Goal Realization Self Help Guide.**

Exercising to explore goal realization can help you discover you. While you may think I am asking you to visit the gym, exercise extends further. What I mean is that you must exercise your brain to find answers, explore possibilities and the like. So get off those running shoes and pull up a chair, since you are going to start by relaxing.

Exercise:

Did you know that the way you think revolves around how you see things, what you hear, smell, taste, and breathe? Likewise, how you think affects your mentality overall. Thus, the mind has to have moderate levels of oxygen to perform comfortable. Thus, when the mind is bottled down it is taking oxygen and requires you to take breaths and relax to bring the oxygen level back up. Now, let's consider the exercise that leads to goal realization:

Sit in a comfortable chair, sitting up straight. Relax and hold your head upward or straight while looking ahead. Cup your hands in your lap without crossing them. Now, while in position close your eyes, allow the body, and mind to feel at ease. If you notice tension in the body areas, let it go. Now take a few deep breathes, inhale, exhale. Make sure you inhale, breathing deep so that it targets the stomach. Once you feel relief, you will next pucker the lips as though you are going to whistle and exhale. Now puff forceful three times to release any other tension. Following the steps again until you reach the count of five, or three if you choose, now observe carefully as your abdomen rises and falls.

Once you are relaxed and finish observing your abdomen move onto allows your thoughts to flow. Think of goals. What do you think, see, hear, and smell, taste, touch, and so forth as you think of goals. I literally think of a woman I spoke with the other day asking me what goals were. I was talking about the subject I was writing and she said, "What are goals." I hope this is not you, since this is an ignorant person out of touch with reality.

To get started set a goal for tomorrow. What are your plans for Memorial Day? Do your plans have areas that could lead to bad consequences? Many people plan to drink in my area on the holiday. Is this your plan? Did you look at the consequences of your plans carefully? Did you plan to stay at home, or employ a designated driver?

Anyway, this is a goal or plan that only lasts a day, but after the day is over you will have other plans to follow. Plans harmonize with goals. If you set goals, you have to write plans to reach your goals. As you start to write, you will discover new ideas, while visualizing self in the moment. This is all part of exercising the brain to set goals, make plans, and achieve the goals.

If you haven't set, goals for self get a calendar. I want you to write each day in that calendar what you plan to do. As you set, the day plans on that day put forth the effort to achieve the daily goal. Continue until one month later you completed all the plans you have written. As you complete the list look back over the daily goals, plans and actions you put forth to achieve the goals. Think of the consequences, actions, feelings, accomplishments and the like. Now think how achieving your daily plans made you feel. Then take out the calendar and set plans for the following month.

Notice what transpired, acceptance, recognizing, awareness, potentials, consequences, exploring, and the like. Exploring then can bring you to realization. Exercising to achieve goal orientation does not involve weights. Is your learning profile in accord with your goals?

Learning Profiles Linking to Goal Realization
Self Help Guide to Success

What have you learnt? What have you learnt can become useful in realizing your goals? What can you use? Knowing how you learn is the start in working toward learning. Thus, if you know what you learnt you have an understanding of what it means to you. If you learnt in your life that we all endure discomforts and that we have to train to tolerate, accept and deal with the discomforts rather than allowing them to hold us down.

Discomforts are natural. We all deal with discomforts at some point in time. Discomforts in fact are a part of our learning procedures. Thus, we have to learn to accept discomforts and allow them to flow freely. Discomforts are obvious when a test or exam is mentioned. Most times people freak out believing they will fail. Instead, these people should let go of their discomforts and practice and prepare to pass the test.

After you learn to deal with discomforts, you should have learnt to match your activities, applying the activities to what you learnt. For instance, if you plan to major in science you would not want to include activities that move away from your goal. Although it is great to take on minor courses that are unrelated, the primary courses you take should revolve around science.

Sometimes you have to adjust what you learnt by using offset strategies. While the rule of thumb for the majority is to learn what they feel comfortable with, or else learn what interest them, thus, learning outside of our interests is a way to open the mind. The steps in school often let us down since time for practicing, integration of meaning and content does not take place, and some teachers fail to deliver content with facts backing it. Rather they will believe what they read and inform the students, and later we find it al was a lie.

Observation is a part of learning and has proven stronger than talking, reading, and the like. In fact, observational therapy is a leading therapeutic strategy that has proven to do more than any other counseling strategy. If you learn observational practices, you will soon learn to watch, listen, and take notes before acting on what you learn. This will also enhance your people skills, which makes life smoother for you. To get started ask self a few questions. Ask what is important to you and what you learn. Ask self what does the topics of interest show you and how does it fit into your plans to achieve your goals.

Now move onto understanding concepts and theories. Concepts could be something imaged or thought of unexpectedly. Concepts go further however, since concepts broad principals that affect perceptions as well as behaviors.

Most times concepts are broad or wide range abstract ideas. Sometimes the concepts are guiding of general principals. For instance, conceptions can determine what you conclude why a person behaves in such a way. Theories are hypothesis, which sometimes a person will conjure up an idea. Theories are assuming, which you want to be careful, since most of the problems we have today are by cause of assuming.

The point is what you learn is how you will understand and relate to your goals. The more you understand and relate the best chance you have of reaching your goal. Still, you need purpose and meaning to achieve your goals.

Finally, I am going to ask you to think about what you learnt, apply it and conduct a research of areas you have concern. Take notes on your new findings and then study your interests again to find meaning. What are the tools that work to see goal realization?

Tools in Goal Realization Self Help Guide

We have tools inside us that we need to cultivate and develop to achieve our goals. Many of the tools we have are obvious, however many fail to see the tools inside them and how they work. This is often because the person has no meaning, purpose, or intentions of understanding the meaning of a single tool, such as values.

Now we can look at a few tools that help us to achieve and considering the meaning as well. Inquisitive is one of the tools we have that help us to learn and achieve. When a person is curious, they will inquire when questions require answers. The person will question things of interest or not while probing into answers to find specifics. Some times inquisitive is not in our favor, especially at what time we become nosy. Those people prying to learn something that does not hold any business to them is nosy and we should never use this tool.

Focusing or awareness is the process of bring focal points to center attractions or interest. If you are focused, you can often get to the heart of the issue while concentrating to learn what it means to you. Focusing helps you to capture moments, expressions, actions and the like you wouldn't ordinary catch while looking straight at the source. As you develop focus skills, you will soon learn to bring your thoughts together more easily.

Willingness is a helpful tool we can use that will take us closer to our goals. A willing person will accept changes good or bad, and will stay keen to each change that comes his way. Willing souls often find life and things learnt enthusiastic, and are often eager to learn. This brings in motivation, thus without motivation you could not reach your goals. Even if you do, it would be a long delay.

Abilities to organize are great working tools that work toward goals. To organize means you can put things I order, by systemizing, arranging, and sorting out. Thus, once you arrange and sort out you can categorize easier and classify what you categorize. It is the process of arranging, controlling, coordinating, and managing. For instance, an organize person can make plans for his goals while taking charge of his life.

Sorting is the process of separating well from bad. Sorting is similar to organized, but it works slightly different, since organizing mixes up ideas to find a variety of notions that leads them to the facts.

Getting it done now is motivation, thus if you get it done now you won't have to worry about it later. For instance, it has bothered me for two days now that a couple of articles delivered to me to complete the batch of articles have issues that disturb me. Therefore, once I write this article I am going to change the information so that it won't bother me anymore. I am getting it done now.

Competency is another tool we can cultivate and develop to work toward goals. Competency means you realize your capabilities, abilities, and skills. Competency also means you stay fit while keeping an aptitude that works with proficiency. This means you have experience and the expertise to use it. For instance, I am armed with words and meanings and I am not afraid to use them.

Joy, most people hear joy and think happy. However, joy means more than happiness, i.e. joy is a happiness that brings us delight and pleasure. Joy is an ecstasy that thrills the heart and brings it to elations to make it move ahead. Keep learning! Develop those tools!

Developing Tools in Goal Realization
Self Help Guide

I spoke of this topic in the past, however I feel it is important to bring this point out strongly, since it is a hinderer or achiever in goal realization. Tools are something we all have inside us. The tools we have require cultivating and developing. Most times people fail to do this, since they often miss the meaning of what the tools do and mean to them.

For instance, did you know that judgment, energy, wellness, self-awareness, willingness, risks, changes, and participating are tools? OK, maybe you recognize the words as inner tools, but maybe you do you know the meaning. I want you to sit for a moment, think of each detail, and draw a meaning to focus. I will practice with you to show what I find, and what it means to me and we can compare to see if we grip the same meaning.

Practices:

Judgment Energy Wellness

Self-awareness Willingness Risks

Changes Participating

Now what does it mean. Is it just a list of words without purpose? Let's explore to see what we find.

Judgment: Judgment works in two ways. We can use our judgment to think through situations carefully before concluding results. We can use judgment to assess while reasoning to find facts in opinions, ideas, theories, and the like. We can use our judgment tools to give opinions without stating facts, which means we are using wrongful judgment.

Judgment opens our mind to wisdom, common sense, and intelligence. However, judgment could also lead us to discriminate or reach a verdict.

Energy is our staying power so to speak. Energy gives us force to continue ahead. Energy is our vigor that gives us that get-up-and-go attitude.

Wellness is our physical and mental well-being, which requires nutrition and exercise along with learning good things in life to maintain.

Self-awareness is the process of knowing oneself well. It is a balance view of self. Self-awareness is an honest point of view of self, and an ability to use interactions with others, while speaking frankly and with confidence.

Willingness is the ability to accept changes, take risks, and participate in life. Willingness is a ready person enthused about what he could learn.

Willingness is motivation that keeps the mind keen and complaint. Willingness is eagerness to move ahead.

Risks could mean that you are willing to take a change on something of interest with odds for you or against you. For instance, you might decide to bungee jump knowing that injuries, loss, or damage could exist. Taking out insurance policies holds risks to you and the policyholder for instance. You can never tell if an insurance provider will hold up to his end in the event you suffer loss. Another example of risks is buying a new home without knowing for sure if you have the money in the future to pay for the home. We all take risks in life.

Change is the biggest hinderer in the world. Changes include alterations, modifications, and transformations. Changes can mean varies in life, or revolutionizing. Change could also mean adjustments and amends. Most of all change means difference. Difference is what terrifies the majority of human beings, thus hindering them from achieving their goals. Difference then is change that leads to diversity and discrepancy.

Participating is the process of contributing something of self, such as time to others. It is the process of partaking in activities, recreation, education, and the like by chipping in your two cents. Participating is also joining and involving self to learn and grow to accept difference.

Now sit down and write the meanings and review to see how they apply to you. You can study to learn you, which is a step closer to goal realization.

Studying to Learn You in Goal Realization
Self Help Guide to Success

I am courageous. I am a generalist that is interested in many understandings of life. I am willing to accept changes, risks, and paradox. I am self-directing and spontaneous at the right moment, and relaxed about my progresses in life. I am intuitive, creative, and willing to feel uncomfortable with emotions as they present self. I am willing to accept all things that come my way, yet I am willing to find the facts at the learning I discover. I am willing to cry, laugh and jump up and down and run down the road when the feeling arises. I am not afraid. I am hungry to learn, and willing to put forth efforts to learn. I am the master of my mind and I am not afraid to use it.

Can you say this? If you can then you, have a better understanding of the person you are and doing better than many others in the world do. In fact, if I were to give statistics of those knowing self and those that do not, I would say 1,000,000,000 to 5. While this is a guess, it still presents some truths if you study human behaviors.

A generalist will explore possibilities. Generalists often use their knowledge, interests, skills, and the like to study and learn a selection of fields. The person is not an expert in a single field, yet he is an expert in all fields.

A person willing to accept changes, risks, and paradox is willing to learn with an open mind. Paradox is someone willing to view contradictions, irony, illogicality, and the like to search for potential truths.

If you are self-directing this means, you are ready and willing to learn and act on your learning without concerning self with punishment and rewards.

Creative souls often go beyond the normal minds, since they draw images, create new ideas, and consider all possibilities even if it does not make sense to you. For instance, there is no proof that dragons exist, yet a creative mind will use his past stories to tell a story while using a dragon to reach a point.

Courageous souls are those brave hearts that speak boldly and assertively to make their points. The courageous souls are spirited in nature and refuse to go against their beliefs once firmly grounded. Courageous souls are not pusillanimous.

Spontaneous is a good quality when boundaries and limits are set. If you are spontaneous at all times, you will land in some serious problems somewhere along your past. Some people at the spontaneous act on their thoughts and later learn they made a mistake. Some people learn to use their natural impulses to act. Still, few people have no boundaries that cause impulsive, unprompted actions. This leads to unplanned and unstructured lives.

Therefore, it is important to control your spontaneous tool and use it when it applies.

Overall goal realization is the process of learning self and understanding what you can do as a person. If you have the ability to change, accept changes you are one-step ahead of the rest of the world. Likewise, if you have the ability to accept differences, cultures, ethnics, race, groups, different opinions and the like, you are one-step ahead of the rest of the world.

To understand more about goals I recommend that you sit down, relax, and write down a few of your qualities. Study the qualities carefully to see what it means to you. Think about the qualities and decide where they fit into goal realization. Relationships and goal realization is another of the considerations we want to ponder over.

Relationships and Goal Realization
Self Help Guide

Entering a relationship with someone whether it is friendship, love, commitment, and so forth can bring on stress and hinder us from seeing our goals. Most times people have plans and goals they haven't fulfilled before joining in a new relationship. This opens the door to chaos, especially if the person meets someone that is not seeking the same goals. At this point, it's all about acceptance. Some people start up relationships with the intentions of achieving particular goals with the second party. At what time you set goals for the two of you, it is important that those goals work in harmony. In fact, you should discuss with your partner, friend, etc the goals you wish to achieve. If the party is willing to participate you have a winning hand, however, if the party has a different plan you have to work together still to help each other achieve.

A goal where more than one party is involved is known as Joint Venturing (JV). The two put a plan in action that works in harmony with each other's intentions. Thus, the plan often

158

remains on track and the two jointly and similar work in union. For instance, when a couple marries, the man will bring in the bacon while the wife takes care of the home. Now the wife works with her husband, since she will help with financial obligations, raising the children, keeping the family well, and working in other areas to help both of the parties involved reach their goals.

To get along with each other in relationships you have to come to agreements. Sometimes it has to be the other person's way and sometimes it can be your way. The primary goal is to understand goals itself, along with what the goals mean to you. For instance, the primary goal of us all is to survive, therefore you have a connection already established with your joint ventured partner.

Using when people join in relationships were love and commitment is involved they often start on the wrong foot. The first goal is to learn the person before deciding to commit to the person. If the two would court without joining in sexual relations first and then marry, they would stand a better chance of survival.

The point is while joining in relationships you have to consider goals on both sides of the fence. If you consider both sides, you can work your goals to work in harmony. Working in harmony means you have an agreement established. The best solution is learning each other's needs and wants before setting harmonized goals. This will help you to see clearer as to which direction you are heading.

As you move along, learn to respect each other. Respect means to avoid doing things that could hurt the other person. This will help you achieve your goals and stay in accord as a partner. To help you come to a realization consider the possibilities.

What do you want from your future and relationship? What does your partner want from her/his future and the relationship? How does both of you intend to work to achieve those goals? DO you want a new home in the next five years? Will both of you work together to achieve this goal? If you are considering friendship, consider.

What does your friend contribute to helping you achieve your goals? Does your friend interfere with your plans to reach your goals? Does your mate interfere with your plans to reach your goals? Keeping asking questions and eventually you will come up with goal realization.

Pondering to Discern Goal Realization
Self Help Guide

Do you ponder to understand your goals? Sometimes we consider goals and beat our heads in the wall trying to figure out which direction we want to go. The problem is we use emotions to reach conclusions instead of our head. If you consider all details of what you want from life, you will soon learn new ideas. Pondering is thinking over situations while contemplating and deliberating new ideas, old ideas, experiences, consequences, and the like.

Pondering is the process of wondering what could happen while brooding over the possibilities and consequences.

Life is full of surprises. Life brings us shock, revelations, disclosures, blows, bombshells, and shockers. Life could astonish you, amaze you, flabbergast you, or stun you to shock. Life can take the wind from your breath, and leave you dazed and dumbfounded. Life brings us many surprises. If you learn to accept life's changes, you will develop keenness, awareness while focusing on your goals.

If you ponder with awareness, you will soon reach conclusions. Conclusions an end to issues and closes the mind from wondering, worrying or doubting. Conclusions also terminates and finales decisions while closing the stages that lead to the conclusion.

Practice:

Use deductions to debate a problem you had recently Use assumptions while searching for facts

Now base your findings on your suppositions Now draw a conclusion on your learning

Understanding is essential in goal realization. If you have understanding, you will find meaning and purpose of your goals. To learn to understand you need to practice thinking, consideration, sympathy, appreciations, indulgent, perceptions, and tolerance. Now use your knowledge to comprehend and bring it to insights. Meaning backs values, worth, and sense.

Practice:

Value: Question: What are your values?

Worth: Question: What is your worth? What do your goals mean to you? Sense: Do you use common sense. Practice listening to your intuitions and go with them.

Meaning: What significance do you goals have? What are the consequences of planning, acting, and reaching your goals? What is the value of your goals? What implications in your plans bring forth the worth of your goals? Have you set your goals? What are you plans?

As you grow to ponder without relying on the emotions, you will soon develop skills that will help you achieve your goals. Still, you want to consider feelings that come from emotions. Emotions overall are feelings, passions, drives, sensations, or sentiments. Feelings extend further. Feelings cause reactions. Feelings are our opinions, point of views, beliefs, views, considerations, and impressions.

Feelings can bring out suspicious, intuitions, ideas, hunches, and act on gut reactions. Since inclinations come from the heart we can see feelings is the heart reactions. Now you might ask what does this have to do with goal realization, however I am going to let you ask and let you figure it out self.

Practice:

What are your feelings about your goals? What are your feelings about life? What do you feel that is interesting to you? What meaning do your feelings present? What purpose belongs to you? What are your intuitions telling you? What is your mood? How do you express your emotions?

If you want goal realization, you have to work hard to get it. Goal realization does not hit the brain over night; rather it takes time to unearth variants of you that uncover goal realization. Now if you want goals you will need to discover your wants first and move ahead in accordance while understanding your qualities and pondering on new ideas. You will need to employ your experience to get what you want.

Goal Realization and What it means to you
Self Help Guide in Success

You could set goals all day long but if you do not have purpose or meaning what would it mean to you? Goals are successes and accomplishes we achieve unconsciously or consciously. To help you understand goals, and how it works we can consider the basics.

The basics goals in life include getting through elementary. Next to follow is central and then high school. Once you finish high school, you begin to consider the college you will attend. You start to go through a chain of changes, which sometimes makes it difficult to decide. You start college and go for a year or two before you realize what you want from your career.

Once you get through with college, you move into a career.

This is where people often stay most times, however some people move further to open a goal to start their own business. Some people are satisfied working for others. Still, once the job is situated people often move toward establishing credit further, buying a home, marrying, and starting a family.

Now, I want you to take a test and decide where you are at with your goals and where you intend to go with your goals.

Are you finished with college? Do you have a career? Is the career fulfilling? Does it have meaning? What is your purpose? Do you intend to start a business in the future? Do you know what this entails?

Ok, say you are intending to start a business in five years. What do you have written in your plans to achieve the goals? In other words, what actions, and efforts do you intend to use to achieve the goals? What are the consequences? Once you open the business, are you prepared for the changes that come along with the business?

For instance, are you considering insurance? Do you consider overhead, costs, expenses, and the like while planning to achieve your goal? What type of business do you intend to open? What is the meaning? What is your purpose?

Establishing meaning and purpose could put you on home base. If you learn your meaning and purpose, you have a clearer path to your future. Therefore, when you plan and set goals make sure that you consider all details of your plans. For instance, I intend to open a business in five years. What does it include? What will it hold for my future? What are the financial obligations? Can I manage my budget to meet these expenses? Do I have a backup plan incase my ultimate plan fails?

Setting goals provide us ambition. Goals take us to objectives, aims, and targets in life. Goals provide us hope and provide us the desire to achieve. Goals are our wants and wishes in life. As you can see, setting goals is important. If you do not set goals, you will miss hope, fulfillment, completeness, and the like. In other words, if you do not have goals you will not fulfill your desires and wants, thus incompleteness creeps in. Now think of your wants.

Practice:

What do I desire?

What is it I wish for in life?

What would I like? What do I crave?

What do I yearn for and what am I hankering after? What are my requirements?

What do I need?

What aspires me? What is my aim?

Now consider what the downside of goals is, i.e. considering what not setting goals, finding meaning and purpose leads.

Think of:

Poverty Famine Hunger Need Neediness Lack Absence Dearth

Keep thinking until you get the point. How do you work toward goal realization?

How to Work Toward Goal Realization
Self Help Guide

The last of all articles on goal realization has reached his final point. NOT! Goal realization articles will continue throughout our lifetime telling you how to realize your goals. Still, it takes you to realize.

How goal realization works depends on you. Goal realization depends on the effort, achievements, and accomplishments you have earned already to apply toward your goal. Even if you haven't established a goal, your achievements, efforts, and accomplish can apply to your future goals, thus to help you see how to establish goals we can consider a few details.

Do you tell the truth even if it hurts? If so then you have a quality to achieve goals.

DO you work with smaller changes and go through larger changes? Then you have an ability to prosper.

DO you affirm changes, actions, words, thoughts, plans, and the like? If so then you are accomplishing your goals.

Do you commit to what you do? If so then you have a strong commitment to achieve in life.

Do you seek support and feedback? Then you have the ability to learn.

Next, we want to work with your beliefs. IF you do not believe that telling the truth will set you free, then you will hinder self from goals. Do you believe the truth will set you free?

Do you believe changes are positive reflections on your life? If you believe this, you have the ability to accept changes.

Do you believe that affirming your goals, plans, decisions, habits, behaviors, and the like can empower you to move forward? If so then you have a strong belief that will lead you to success.

Do you believe that commitment is a part of life that we all have to learn sometime in our life? Stop here, since commitments often terrorize people, since it is a change. Commitments are obligations or pledges that you will do something. Now you can say you will do something but putting forth the action to do it makes you an honest person. What fear is in this consequence? Nothing, thus do you realize that commitment is loyalty, allegiance, duties, responsibility, and liability. Liability is what terrorizes people unknowingly and unwittingly.

170

Continuing, do you believe that seeking support and feedback can help you grow? If so then continue seeking support and feedback, since it will help you grow.

Now consider writing down your idea goals. Even if you are unsure, write it down. If you are not good at writing, use the computer to type in your goals, or possible goals. As you write or type your potential goals, consider ideas, since ideas are tools that help you grow and become aware.

Next, take out your calendar. Write down your daily activities. Write the most important activities and work toward the least activity. Continue this process for one month and review once the month has finished. Now, write another daily plan and work to achieve those goals. Work one day at a time until you can work toward writing 5 year, 10 year, 20 years, or 50-year plans. The more you practice writing and carrying out your plans, even if it is one day at a time you will finally grow into writing goals that include long-term.

Now, visualize self in five years. What do you see yourself doing this? Do you believe you can do this? Visualize self in ten years and follow the same procedure. Continue to practice as you move along, so that you can grow into goal realization. Practice makes your life better, so keep practicing.

CONCLUSION

Goals are terminal points that lead to a race in life. Goals should be easily set and achieved, thus while setting goals you want to keep logic in mind. If you set goals out of your reach, it is likely you will never reach the end of the race. Setting goals out of your reach will also frustrate you. Thus, at what time you continue to fail you will loose self-esteem, self-control, confidence, and all mechanisms that make you a complete human being. The overall point is to set goals where you can win the race. To help you we can look at a few strategies.

Printed by Libri Plureos GmbH in Hamburg, Germany